C

# CONTACT ON GORKY STREET

Oleg Penkovsky and Greville Wynne

Greville Wynne

# CONTACT ON
# GORKY STREET

*New York*  ATHENEUM  *1968*

# Contents

# Illustrations

# Preface

It is only now that I feel the time has come when I can write a book about my work with Penkovsky. I have not done so before because I wanted to be quite sure that my friend Oleg Penkovsky was not alive and that by writing a book I would not make things more difficult for him. He was sentenced to death, but the sentence was not carried out. It was nearly two years later that I learnt how Penkovsky, imprisoned for further interrogation in a remote village, had taken his own life.

The reader might well ask, 'What has this operation achieved?' It should be understood that I was not engaged in the operation as an expert in the economical, political or military field. My job, as I have explained in these pages, was to keep the pipe-line open. From my many talks with Penkovsky, from a sight of some of the material which passed through my hands, and from other observations, I conclude that the following was amongst the information that Penkovsky gave to the West:

1. The names—amongst them Lonsdale's—and in many cases photographs of over 300 Soviet agents working in Western countries. In addition, several hundred agents under training in the Soviet Union, Czechoslovakia and other Eastern countries were made known to the West,

together with the names and details of Western National-
ists who are in the pay of or in league with the Soviet
Communists. Penkovsky, in fact, dealt a crippling blow to
the Soviet espionage system. After his arrest Serov, head
of the Soviet Intelligence Service, was dismissed.

2. Details of the Soviet rocket sites throughout the
Soviet Union, together with statistical details of training
manpower, weapon production, stock-piling and drawing
board designs for future programmes. After Penkovsky's
arrest Marshal Varentsov, in charge of rocket defences,
was dismissed.

3. Penkovsky passed on the information that Khrushchev had allowed most important control equipment, which
was in very short supply, to be sent with rockets to Cuba.
Khrushchev had gambled on leaving the Soviet defence
system denuded, in order to provide a showpiece in Cuba
for Soviet propaganda.

4. Penkovsky photographed reports which Khrushchev
had given to the Soviet Praesidium, purporting to be an
account of a meeting between Kennedy and himself, and
the Italian Foreign Minister and himself. When Kennedy
saw these reports, he found that they were very different
from the meetings that had actually taken place. Accord-
ingly, true copies of the minutes of the meetings were sent
to the Praesidium. Not so long after Penkovsky's arrest
Khrushchev was dismissed.

5. Statistics of agricultural production throughout the
Union, showing the inefficiency in fullest detail. Since then,
the 'collective farming' system has been de-centralised.
Agricultural factories are now responsible for their own
products instead of being controlled from Moscow.

6. Production figures, location, lay-out and operating
procedures for all the main Soviet industries, including
the electronics industry, and the production of steel, aircraft and military equipment.

7. Considerable information dealing with the Soviet Union's relations with Eastern European countries; photostatic copies of secret agreements; details of future policy of the Soviet Government towards those countries,

information that could hardly have failed to strengthen the Western Powers in their dealings with Communist Russia. All in all, Penkovsky helped to make it impossible for the Soviet Union to continue its bluff. The result has been a complete change of political climate, a more realistic approach to common problems between the Soviet Union and the West, and certainly in the last year or two a genuine desire on the Soviet side for more friendly relations. There is less talk of 'submerging the West with rockets', and more talk of pacts and economical alliance.

I must acknowledge the encouragement in writing it which I have received from many friends and colleagues.

My grateful thanks go to John Gilbert who, as a professional writer, has given me his generous help and advice.

GREVILLE WYNNE

# I

# Capture

## I

V AROS LIGET PARK, Budapest.

There was a pale light in the sky and a great stillness. As I came down the pavilion steps with Ambrus, I felt a stab of danger. The palms of my hands were wet. And I knew why. Because the Hungarian delegates whom I had been entertaining for the last two hours had suddenly, as if on order, left the party. They had melted away, leaving me alone with Ambrus. He was my interpreter. I had never trusted him, but there was no choice.

Many times in the past eighteen months I had felt danger, and for stronger reasons, but the thing I feared had not yet happened. The moments had come and gone, and this was probably another. As we walked down the steps, Ambrus asked me where I was dining and I said I did not know, and Ambrus said there was a nice little place up in Buda with an Italian dancer. He made suggestive curves with his hands and laughed in a coarse way, and to my super-alerted mind this seemed like a clumsy attempt to distract me. But I did not run away. There was really nowhere to run to. I could see my caravans not a hundred yards away under the trees, and I knew I would never reach them.

They were beautiful caravans, built to my own design for trade exhibitions. There was a motorised unit and a trailer, each with two compartments for exhibiting tools and machine equipment. That was the official purpose of the caravans. The unofficial purpose was to give me one more excuse for going to Russia to see Oleg Penkovsky, and if possible to bring him out.

London (I mean those I worked for) were very anxious to save Penkovsky. A concealed space had been built big enough for a man to lie down. This had been made overnight, on pretext of road tests, by workmen nothing to do with the engineers who had built the caravans for exhibitions. The caravans cost over £35,000. London would have spent ten times that amount to save Penkovsky.

It was a good party. The manager of the Duna Hotel organised the food and drink and I showed off the caravans and introduced the English representatives to the Hungarians. The English firms were pleased to have their equipment shown in Budapest, and London was pleased because if the Budapest exhibition were a success it would be a step towards the Soviet Union.

Everyone I had asked to the party had come. With one exception. The Commercial Secretary at the British Embassy had sent one of his minor officials. This was not good, but I was used to it. All over the world British trade suffers from the attitude of the embassies towards the sordid necessities of commerce. Large official groups, provided they give months of warning, would be welcomed by the embassies with a stately if somewhat Victorian ceremony, but individual businessmen relying on their extempore initiative have a rugged time. But in spite of the Commercial Secretary's aloofness the party had gone well. We started at five o'clock and for two hours gallons of liquor had disappeared in the good cause, and then suddenly, when evening was coming quickly in the pale sky, the Hungarians melted away. The English executives were still standing by in their compartments, and I was alone with Ambrus among the empty bottle-laden tables.

At the bottom of the steps I turned to speak to Ambrus, but he had gone. I saw him across the driveway. Between him and me four men had appeared as if by magic. They were all short and thickset and wore their trilby hats at the same angle. One of them said quietly: 'Mr. Veen?' and I said, 'Yes, that is my name' and then, with the danger filling me, I shouted to Ambrus and he called back, 'It's all right, they speak good English,' and walked away. If I had run they would have shot me. A saloon had drawn up beside us. It was the Russian-built Moskovich. There was another car by the entrance gates. I was tripped and my arms were seized. The back door of the front car was opened and I was hurled inside. As I fell head first I grabbed the far handle and opened the door and yelled to my driver, Charles. He was standing by the caravans. I had been trained that, if and when this thing happened, I must at any cost let someone know. I yelled at the top of my voice and in the second before the door was slammed against my head I saw Charles swing round and wave and start running towards the car. Then I was kicked in the kidneys by heavy feet and something metal hit my temple.

That was about seven o'clock on Friday the 2nd November 1962.

When I came to I was wedged in the bottom of the car, my hands handcuffed behind me, feet on my back, and blood all over my face. The car was moving and when several minutes later it stopped I was dragged out half conscious and hauled through the gates of a prison. In a dirty room behind a dirty desk lit by a shaded lamp sat a dirty civilian. I was still dazed, but I saw that they had ripped off the lapels of my jacket. Lapels are where agents hide poison. The civilian sprawled in the chair, picking his nose.

'So you are Mr. Veen?'

'Yes.'

'Why do you spy on us?'

'I don't know what you are talking about.'

'Ha!'

He was filthy, unshaven, and looked as if he had not been to bed for a week. For a full minute he stared at me. Then he gave an order in Russian and I was stripped naked. With a torch and a metal probe they examined every orifice in my body. They were not gentle, and some orifices hurt more than others.

That was the beginning of their long attempt to degrade me. It was also the moment when I started to despise them. I despised them for daring to think they could degrade me and also because they themselves were so slovenly and dirty.

More than my training, more than love of my country, even more than thoughts of my home, it was this fury of contempt which in the end saved me. Day and night for the next eighteen months I was to generate such loathing for these caricatures of humanity, such unbelief that they could impose their will on the people of Russia, still less on the world, and least of all on myself, that at last, though I was still their prisoner, their power over me was totally destroyed.

The man stopped picking his nose and told me to dress. The four guards in the room were all armed. I was taken to a cell with a double door, a barred window, a metal bed with hard mattress, and no food. I must have slept, for the night passed quickly, but it seemed to me that I was lying horribly awake. The blood on my head and face had dried, but I had nothing to wipe it off with except my spittle and handkerchief. My head throbbed. It was clear that I could not get out of the cell and I knew logically that there would never be a chance of escape as long as the Russians wanted to keep me. But I could still not believe that I was a prisoner and would stay a prisoner. I kept thinking that at any moment the door would open and I would be rescued by the British

Minister. Charles must have told someone. There would be official protests. It was all a misunderstanding.

I knew a man who worked on a band-saw. One day he was careless and the next moment he was looking at his own hand lying in the sawdust with blood pouring out of his stump. He said that for at least a minute he stared at his hand and did nothing. He could see his hand, his own hand that belonged to him and no one else, lying there motionless, and it seemed to him utterly impossible that this was reality. It must be some flash of absurd and momentary imagination. It could not really have happened.

This was how I felt that night about being a prisoner of the Russians. . . .

Next morning I was taken by Soviet Military aircraft to Moscow. I was handcuffed. There were ten armed soldiers in the plane, and an interpreter and several officers and a woman doctor who bandaged my head. Again I had to admit that escape was improbable. I suppose that James Bond would have spat from his mouth a gas capsule (concealed in his molar) which would have overcome everyone but himself and would then have leapt to safety with a parachute concealed up his backside. But I regret to reveal that the British Intelligence Service lags behind Bond in ingenuity.

So I told myself that at Moscow Airport the British Ambassador would undoubtedly be waiting.

He was not.

Instead there was a line of armed soldiers, several Alsatians and a black prison van. It was evening and I had still not eaten. I could not see out of the van, but when we stopped, and I was taken through the gates of a prison built on a hillside, I knew where I was.

Lubyanka! The most famous prison in Russia. Many times in my days of freedom, strolling with Penkovsky through the streets of Moscow, I had seen the outside of those grim walls.

Now I was to see the inside.

A lift took me down to my cell. Since I was handcuffed, dazed, weak from hunger, with a gun in my back and six armed soldiers in attendance, the design of the lift seemed unnecessarily elaborate. It was made of steel and there was a spring-lock on the door. At the back of the lift was a smaller door, and when I was thrust inside I found myself in a cramped space, squeezed in a standing position, with my face against a spy-hole through which I could see nothing but the face of the soldier who was taking me down. The others had stayed in the corridor above. Down, down and down.

It was probably less than a minute but it seemed like an hour. That slow sinking journey was the end of my hope. The image of the British Ambassador faded from my mind like a child's drawing wiped from the slate. I knew only too well what happened to agents caught by the Russians. I was an agent and my training had been thorough and explicit.

My cell had a metal bed, too heavy to move, a tiny high window and a tepid radiator. I was left for an hour, then taken up to the interrogation room before a general, a lieutenant-colonel and interpreter.

We were perfectly polite to each other. The General said he knew all about me and it was just a question of my signing a confession. I said I did not know what he was talking about. We repeated this simple exchange several times. Then I was taken to another room and my baggage from the Duna Hotel was brought in. The contents were tipped on to a table and there were many questions about my toilet accessories (unknown in Russia) most of which I answered truthfully. But when it came to the bottle of Tokay wine I told in a sudden flicker of temper a lie. The bottle was squat and long-necked. The wine was thick and golden. It had been given to me by a Hungarian Trade Minister. When the interpreter asked me what it was I said: 'Shampoo.' The Corporal made a slow, grave entry on the inventory and the bottle was taken away with all my other belongings. The bottle came back to me seven months later in circumstances which I could never in my most inventive moments have foreseen.

Back in my cell I was given my first food for twenty-four hours. A mug of weak tea without milk, a bowl of thin soup, and some black bread. I made it last as long as I could. I knew that ahead of me stretched endless empty hours. They would have to be filled, and only my own resources would fill them. I knew that all my training and discipline would be necessary to withstand the terrible weight of emptiness.

So as a beginning I paid deliberate and slow attention to every moment of mastication, every act of swallowing. When the last crumb and drop were beyond recall I sat on my bed and listened to the clicking of a shutter on the spy-hole in my door. The guard passed regularly but I could not hear his footsteps because there was a drugget laid outside the cell door and the guards all wore soft slippers. All I could hear was the clicking of the shutter. It was like the ticking of a clock grotesquely retarded. A monstrous great-grandfather clock whose pendulum swung only once every two minutes. A clock whose snail-like mechanism would record the months, maybe the years. London had warned me to be prepared for five years. It was impossible to apprehend such a length of time.

I sat on my bed and said the alphabet very slowly. It was important to use the brain so that the mind would not be free to worry. Left to itself the mind would fly to dangerous subjects, to things and people whose loss was so terrible that to dwell on it would bring despair and madness. The mind was in fact a sentimental baby. So after the alphabet I started reciting all the films I could remember and many other statistical recollections, but always, behind whatever I was thinking or saying, there hovered a single figure, the person for whom, by whom and with whom I had been deeply occupied for over six years. The bravest man I had ever met. A great Russian, a great patriot.

Oleg Penkovsky, colonel in the Red Army, a senior member of the Communist Party, high in the Russian Military Intelligence Service, perhaps the most valuable agent who ever came to the West.

Where was he now?

## II

This is not a mystery story. There are excitements enough without my trying to conceal 'who done it', so let me say at once that Oleg Penkovsky was the man who, because he was a great patriot, because he loved the Russian people and hated their rulers, assembled a vast file of topmost Soviet secrets, military, economic and political, whose revelation would, he hoped, enable the Western powers to contain and even to overthrow the tyranny of his country; and I was the agent, chosen and trained by British Intelligence (with what thoroughness you will see), who first made contact with Penkovsky, who arranged for him to bring his secrets to London, who, when excuses for him to leave Moscow could not be found, brought the secrets out myself, who for eighteen months was his close accomplice in Moscow, England and Paris, who became—and I claim this with pride—his friend.

Oleg, or 'Alex' as he liked me to call him, was a great companion, fond of good living, always well dressed (a rarity in the Soviet Union), and physically very strong. Once when my car jack broke he held up the side of the Humber saloon for five minutes while I changed the wheel. His eyes, clear and deep-set, were magic to women. He had a straight back and a quick walk, and always kept himself in first-class condition.

'No, Greville, taxis are bad for you. Let us walk.' And to walk with Alex meant exercise.

We had much in common. I, born in March 1919, was a month the older, and he, at five foot eight, was slightly the taller. Both our fathers had been mining engineers. We both had military and Intelligence training, and our tastes were very similar. We smoked, but not heavily, and we preferred beer and wine to spirits, even vodka. We liked good food well served and, though we believed in discipline, we were neither of us nine-to-five men. When there was work to do we did it, and when it was finished we liked the lights to be bright. It was always fun with Alex, and when in the end I saw his wonderful vitality destroyed by the men he hated I felt an inexpressible shame, as if liberty herself had been mauled.

Often I had been asked the question: 'But Penkovsky was born a Russian. Therefore, whatever his feelings about the government, was he not a traitor to give away secrets that might threaten his country?'

My answer is this:

'We live in a democracy, and the governments which come and go, which we have the power to eject, are temporary teams endeavouring to deal with our problems by methods that differ but slightly. Whether Socialists or Tories are in power, to give away our secrets would be a betrayal of the freedom we take for granted. Too much for granted, in my opinion.

'But supposing Britain were shanghaied by a gang of criminals who, once in power, could never constitutionally be thrown out? Suppose that to raise your voice against the government meant life imprisonment or death? Suppose we had secret police and no free elections? Would you still say that to work against the government was an act of treason?'

Penkovsky thought not, and I agree with him.

For years he worked alone, unable to share his plans with a living soul, and from the moment he was first noticed by

British Intelligence it was more than five years before I was able to make contact with him. It is a story of patience and foresight in high degree. This is how it happened.

In the summer of 1955 Colonel Oleg Penkovsky was the Assistant Soviet Military Attaché in Ankara. He was, besides, Senior Assistant in the Chief Intelligence Directorate of the Red Army, the G.R.U.

For Penkovsky in Ankara the social life was ready-made. He had an attractive wife and was welcome in the narrow circle of Soviet functions. His official work was not arduous and the evenings were filled with parties and receptions. A gay and somewhat exhausting life, to which Colonel Penkovsky reacted in a manner strictly against the Soviet rules. He formed the habit of slipping away alone for a stroll round the city or a glass of wine at one of the pavement cafés. If a junior officer had done this he would immediately have been in trouble. Soviet staff were expected to maintain their own society. Penkovsky was high enough up to explain his excursions, had any superior challenged him, but there was one person in Ankara whose duty was not to challenge but to observe.

A British Intelligence agent saw the Russian colonel sitting alone, saw the glass pause between table and lips, noted not once but on many evenings the faraway expression—and told London. And London, sensitive to the smallest oddities of behaviour, paused to reflect.

It might mean nothing. A man was certainly free to have a drink alone, though a Soviet officer was less free than most. But why so often? And why no companion? Penkovsky was known to have a roving eye, so why no girl? And why the faraway expression? Might it, could it not, suggest a restlessness? A dissatisfaction? An intention perhaps?

It was little enough to go on, but it was enough. From this seed of observation arose the greatest act of prevision in the

history of espionage, for London decided that if and when—
no matter how long it took or where it occurred—Penkovsky
wanted to give information, whatever it might be, then he
would find at his elbow someone to whom he would naturally,
without suspicion, turn for help and co-operation.

Great delicacy was needed. Anything like a frontal approach to Penkovsky at this stage was impossible. Perhaps,
if he had stayed longer in Ankara, an agent might have been
sent to develop a slow acquaintance which would later prove
useful. But now Colonel Penkovsky was transferred back to
Moscow, where he joined the 4th Directorate of Military
Intelligence. Reports from our agents showed that his behaviour pattern was still the same, and now the problem was
to insert the right man at the right time into Moscow itself.

No regular British agent existed in the Soviet Union who
was in the sort of position that might cross or have any connection with Penkovsky's career as an army officer. A regular
agent, who might in any case be already known and marked
by the Russians, could not move around to fit in with
Penkovsky's movements without creating the most obvious
suspicion.

Someone new was needed. Someone who could travel in
the Union without suspicion; who would be accepted at his
face value for some bona-fide work that he could be doing in
Russia; who could be steered towards Penkovsky at the right
time; who would not know till the last moment what his real
mission was—since a perfectly natural behaviour could be
achieved better by ignorance than by acting; and who, when
he did know what was required, would have the experience
to do whatever was necessary to assist Penkovsky.

The obvious choice was a businessman, preferably one
who had already travelled extensively, so that an entry into
the Union would seem natural. There were plenty such men,
but they were not trained for Intelligence, and no crash pro-

gramme could give a man what he would most need in a crisis—experience.

So London wanted someone who had already worked for them, who had proved himself an agent, and who now, ten years after the war, was established in some acceptable field of international commerce.

The man they chose was me.

My first contact with British Intelligence was by accident in 1938. I was at that time a student apprentice in electrical engineering, attending lectures at University College in Nottingham, and doing practical work in a large local factory. I had been working at the factory one afternoon on a cable in an underground compartment of a storehouse. Late that evening in my apartment I found that I had left some of my tools in the storehouse. Since early next morning I was to visit another factory out of town I decided to retrieve the tools. The night watchman at the factory gates showed no surprise on my arrival, for at this period of time I was working on factory maintenance when the factory plant had closed down; nightwork and weekend work was not unusual.

The storehouse was large and full of crates and packing cases. I opened the door and slipped inside. Why so quietly? An instinct from childhood, I think. My mother had taught me that you didn't bang about in the middle of the night. She little foresaw the result of her training, for if I had banged that door this story would never have happened.

The tools were lying against the wall near the door, and I was about to turn on the light when I heard a voice. It came from the far end of the cellar, and the words I recognised as German. Slowly, step by step, I felt my way down the avenue of crates, till suddenly in a small pool of light I saw a man sitting with his back to me. His body hid what was on the bench, but rising above his shoulder I could see an aerial. I immediately thought that this could very well be an illegal communication point with Hitler's Germany, for I could not see any permissible reason for a man transmitting from a cellar in the middle of the night.

I crept back, collected my tools near the entrance, and returned to my apartment. Next evening, after my factory visit, I decided to make a report. But to whom?

The natural person would have been the head of the firm. He was a first-rate man who had always treated me well, but some instinct told me to be very careful. I did not know what 'security' really meant, but I had a feeling that this might be important. There was another member of the firm who seemed to me more suitable for this sort of confidence. He was an ex-army colonel whom I had spoken to many times because he also lectured at the local O.T.C. and I had heard that in the Great War he had been connected with the Intelligence branch.

He listened carefully, told me not to speak to anyone else about the matter and early the next evening he took me to see a man who proved to be a director of Intelligence. I was congratulated on my sense of security, and told that my surmise was correct.

A few days later the Colonel discussed with me my feeling about the militia call-up, as I was of the age-group for the first call. He asked me if I had decided on which branch of the service I was entering. At the time I was young, eager, inquisitive and very fond of my country. I told him I would be willing to work in any branch of the service where I would do most good, but preferably where also my engineering training would be put to some use. No immediate comment was made. Again I was thanked for what I had done.

Some weeks later the Colonel came to me at the works and told me that I would be given a special interview, which would have considerable bearing on my future call-up for the Army. This interview took place with the director of Intelligence and another colleague. I was told that I would be given the opportunity of some special training before my official call-up to the Armed Services, and, depending on how well I did, special duties might be given me. In September war broke out. I was put into the Army, and almost the whole war I spent in this country. The details may still not be given for security reasons, but my job was, with a variety of ranks and units, to observe and report on enemy agents and suspects in and out of the services. Now I was to put into practice at least three basic principles of Intelligence which I had learnt in training.

First, to behave naturally. Always to act as I would have acted if I had not been an agent. If I were meeting a suspect for a drink and he did not turn up I would not telephone him or go to see where he was any more than I would have fussed over a friend who had missed his pint. If my commanding officer, who would know nothing of my other activities, spoilt my plans with some army errand I would do as I was told. I was a soldier and I must behave as a soldier (just as later in the Soviet Union I behaved as a businessman because I *was* a businessman). This is a fundamental principle of British Intelligence, and it is also the source of a popular misconception. I have heard it said, 'It's a shame, the way they use innocent people to do their dirty work for them.' This is nonsense. No one ever becomes an agent unless he wishes. There is no compulsion, and at every stage you are given the opportunity, as I was given many times, to decline. And the notion of training a citizen to become an agent, instead of vice versa, remains sound. You can train a plumber to be an agent. You could never ask an agent to pretend he was a plumber; he would be certain to give himself away.

Second, to remember details of the man you are observing. Does he smoke? What brand? With a cigarette-holder? Is he left-handed? Has he mannerisms of speech? Or gestures? How does he dress? Any scars, warts, or gold fillings? And his hands. What rings? Any fingers missing? Does he limp?

Does he squint? What does he drink? What books does he read? Does he like redheads or blondes? And the same with places, with streets and rooms. Give me one evening in a man's house and I will tell you more about him and his home than you would notice in ten visits.

Third, that everything matters, whether or not you understand it. When you make a report do not cloud it up with fancy interpretations. Leave that to London. If the agent in Ankara had stopped to ask himself the probable meaning of Penkovsky's solitary tipples he might have concluded they probably meant nothing, and President Kennedy would not have been able to handle Khrushchev as he did over the Cuban crisis.

And now the war is over, and my hand is shaken (literally —not with gold), and I return to civilian life. I become a trader in electrical equipment. Sometimes I represent other firms, sometimes I work alone. I form my own company. I travel to the Far East, to India, and extensively in Europe. I marry Sheila and have a son, Andrew. We find a home in Chelsea. Almost ten years pass, and the war seems long ago, and though I sometimes think of my friends in Intelligence, the men whose Christian names were false and whose surnames I never knew, I do not expect to hear from them again.

And then one morning in the late summer of 1955 my telephone rings, and when I give my name, a voice says, 'James here—remember?' and he adds an address where I did my training—but I remember his voice without the address.

'How are you keeping?' says James.

'Oh, pretty fit.' But I have a feeling that James knows this already.

'Would you care for some lunch today?'

'That sounds a good idea.'

'The Ivy then, at one o'clock.'

It is an excellent lunch. James asks what I have been doing

with myself, but I guess he knows, because when I mention the Far East he says, 'India too, I believe.' He lets me ramble on, and as we are finishing our coffee, he says:

'Why not branch out a bit?'

'Where would you suggest?'

'Well, I don't know, they say business is fairly brisk in Eastern Europe these days,' says James, beckoning the waiter.

That was how it was done. There was no other briefing. I knew that I was being offered an assignment, but when and where it would take place I had no idea. If I had wished to refuse I could have said that Eastern Europe did not interest me. But I accepted, by saying nothing. When the time came I would be told everything; for the moment my mission was to develop my legitimate business in Eastern Europe. Different companies had different footholds, and I varied my choice of company according to where I wanted to go.

I began with Poland. Such visits take time to arrange, and it was not till early the following year that I first went to Warsaw. Returning, my plane was diverted to Prague for which I had no visa. I saw the authorities and was at once granted a temporary permit.

Back in London I was again contacted by James. The Prague episode was known and approved. 'Fine, Greville. Keep it up. And don't be afraid of branching out.' So now I went to other Balkan capitals, to Budapest, Bucharest, Sofia and Belgrade, and always strictly on business. Several times in these cities I was approached by men who would enquire, most discreetly, if I were interested in doing some 'special' work for them, but always I declined, saying that I was first and last a businessman. I knew that whatever London had in store, my only present duty was to build up a genuine and trusted connection in business.

'That's the way, Greville. Keep it up.'

In 1957, at the British Trade Fair in Helsinki, I applied for a visa to the Soviet Union. This I obtained without difficulty, and I went to Moscow for a preliminary survey of business prospects.

I quickly found that the Soviet Union was decades if not centuries behind the Western world in the matter of business procedure. My plan, somewhat vague and elastic, was to introduce into the Union British firms with whose products I was familiar, such as mechanical handling and mining equipment, electronic components, tanning machinery, marine and land power plant, and machine tools. I was not sure how best to establish trade, but I quickly became convinced that it would never be established among the impenetrable scrub of under-secretaries, salesmen and minor officials, most of them women, with whom I was presented. I tried to get higher. I complained to the Soviet Foreign Trade Ministry, but nothing happened. The Soviets are eager for technical information, but highly suspicious of those who offer it. And their ideas of making a foreign businessman welcome are quaint.

For instance.

Staying at the Metropole Hotel, the best in Moscow, whose dining room is a disgrace and whose service is on a par with some no-star hostel in the wilds of Cornwall, I left my car one Sunday morning at the kerb outside the front door. When I returned from visiting Lenin's tomb I found an armed policeman and about a hundred onlookers. The policeman, with the porter as interpreter, explained that my car needed cleaning. So it did. I had driven a long way and the Soviet roads were muddy. It was a penal offence, said the policeman, to have a dirty car in the glorious capital of the Soviet Union. Fair enough, so where could I have my car cleaned? The policeman said there was only one garage in Moscow which was permitted to clean the cars of foreigners.

He told me where this garage was. 'But,' he added impassively, 'it is shut on Sundays.'

I told the porter that I would gladly pay to have my car cleaned by the hotel staff, but the porter said the staff duties did not extend to cleaning foreigners' cars. I said I would get it cleaned tomorrow, when the garage was open, but the policeman said no, I must get it cleaned now, this moment. Well, I could take a hint, I did not need to be kicked in the teeth, so I asked the porter for a bucket of hot water and a rag, and both these being permitted, I was allowed to fetch the bucket myself, and I ended up in my shirt sleeves sluicing down the car while the policeman stood with his hand on his gun and the onlookers laughed and cheered.

I did not complain. Maybe with the engineers I hoped to bring to Moscow I could slip in the manager of an automatic car-wash firm. The Muscovites would surely welcome such an innovation.

I quote the car incident as an example of the astounding backwardness of the Soviets in the amenities of living. Like their ancient lifts, their sordid restaurants, their meagre supply of all consumer goods, their infrequent petrol stations (sometimes up to two hundred miles apart on the open road), their antiquated taxis, their dull clothes, and their almost total unacquaintance with many foods which an East End slum child would take for granted. You would have a job buying a bag of oranges between Moscow and the Black Sea. The Soviet economy is geared for two main objects, scientific progress and military power, just as the political framework is geared for a single object, the continuance of the Communist regime. There is little time or money for amenities.

Though it is none of my present concern, I notice this with sadness, for there is no doubt that the vast mass of Soviet people are warm-hearted, intelligent, and enormously talented. When the state requires opera, or ballet, or musicians, or chess players, or athletes, it can find among its two hundred millions some of the best in the world. But these are state activities, ordered by the Communist Party. It is sometimes not realised what a tiny percentage of the people belong to the Party, and if you are not a Party member, if you are not a scientist or a senior officer or a ballet star, if you are simply one of the tens of millions of ordinary people trying to lead ordinary lives, then your share of the joys of life which the world has to offer is remarkably small.

When I began my business enquiries I was met with a mixture of oriental suspicion and primitive ignorance. For the rest of 1958 and all through 1959 I was dodging to and fro between Moscow, the capitals of Eastern Europe and London trying to set up the market for British products in the Union. The British firms I had in mind were dotted about mostly in the Midlands and the North, and though they understood business procedure better than the Russians, they were hardly less suspicious. All I wanted at this stage were brochures describing their equipment and an assurance that if orders were obtained they would be met. Many were the letters and visits and conferences before I was given even a tentative assurance. I told the British that I had already got permission from the Russians, and I told the Russians that the British were full of enthusiasm. I trusted that this prophetic optimism would come true—which it did, but only after two years of patient negotiation.

'Well, James, I seem to be getting nowhere fast. I don't know which is worse, the Soviet suspicion or the British reluctance. What's the matter with these people? My God, don't they want . . .?'

'Now keep calm, Greville, you're doing fine. Just carry on the way you're going.'

By now I had contacted several Russians in London, mostly connected with their Embassy. I wanted to build up confidence at both ends of the line. Early in 1960 I met a man named Kulikov. I took him to my city office and to the private office in my Chelsea home. I told him of my business activities, and after many questions he sent me to his superior, Pavlov, at the Soviet Embassy. Pavlov was very polite but I knew what he was after. He wanted convincing that I was a genuine businessman, so when he asked if I could arrange for Kulikov and some of his colleagues to visit two or three of the Northern factories I had mentioned, I said, 'I can arrange it now, if I may use your telephone.'

The visit was a great success. When the Kulikov party turned up with second-class tickets I made them change to first class. 'No Western businessman travels anything but first.' So we took a Pullman, and British Railways obliged me with one of their better meals. Our toasts to Anglo-Soviet trade were prolonged.

A few days after our return to London, Kulikov telephoned me to ask for a private meeting, 'But after dark, if you please, Mr. Veen—and not at your house.'

We met on a drizzling evening in the small garden at Chelsea Embankment where the statue of Carlyle gazes across the river. We sat just behind the mighty seer and Kulikov enquired, most delicately and obliquely, if I were willing to sell trade secrets. 'We know you have many friends, Mr. Veen . . . we are interested in all new developments, especially the technical . . . engineering drawings, perhaps . . . you will understand that if such things came into our hands, you would not suffer . . .' His low voice petered into silence. We sat together in the mugginess so special to London. Slow drops of rain fell from the trees on to our hats. I murmured, in a tone which I hoped would convey the glacial surprise shown by British gentlemen through the centuries when confronted with some faintly unethical suggestion from one of the lesser breeds of unprincipled foreigner, 'Mr. Kulikov, I do not know that I quite understand you, but it may answer your question if I say that I am simply and solely a business-man.'

Kulikov did not press his point. After a few pleasantries about our Northern visit he vanished into the rain, and I stepped to where I could look up at Carlyle. 'Incorruptible! Okay?' But the brooding face, wet in the lamplight, continued to gaze across the river.

Early in November 1960 James made his first really concrete suggestion: 'There's an organisation in Moscow called the Scientific Research Committee. They have offices in Gorky Street. It would be interesting for us if you could develop relations with them.'

I had heard of this Committee without realising that, apart from its obvious duties, it also controlled the visits of foreign scientists and engineers. It was typical of Soviet delay that I had not been told of this in Moscow, but now that I knew I hurried back to Moscow and applied for an interview. My application hinted that, instead of merely distributing circulars and prospectuses, I had in mind a more fruitful plan for furthering Anglo-Soviet trade. This hint was necessary because a simple complaint about my activities to date would have been dealt with by a lower authority than the Committee of Scientific Research. The response was immediate. I would be granted an interview.

Number Eleven, Gorky Street, was an imposing building near the Red Square. Armed guards stood in the reception hall and there was a general bustle of messengers and secretaries, at least half of whom were girls. Not pretty girls. The Western business wolf would be disappointed in Moscow. The office girls wear white coats, unironed, and thick low-heeled shoes. Buxom healthy girls, but with bad complexions and no make-up. Brassières and deodorant are unknown to them.

I was greeted by a girl receptionist at a green baize table. The Russians love green baize. They use it everywhere as a symbol of business efficiency, they are delighted with it, as a child delights in the earliest words of his vocabulary.

After several minutes telephoning the girl handed me on to another, who took me to the second floor in a lift. The lift was old and metal, like the luggage lift in a second-rate English hotel, and was prone, as I learnt later, to electrical failure.

I was received, in a long dull room with a long green baize table, by Bodenikov, one of the principals of the Committee. Bodenikov, who spoke excellent English, introduced me to six other men whose names I registered, and when we took our seats mineral drinks were brought and Russian cigarettes. There were two stenographers and a girl interpreter, and from now on Bodenikov spoke only in Russian. He sat at the head of the table and declared the meeting open.

It had been reported, said Bodenikov, that I had complained to the Foreign Trade Ministry. It seemed I had gathered the impression that Soviet authorities were not serious about doing business with the companies I represented. On the contrary, the Soviet Union welcomed genuine trade with all countries. Now what was my new proposal for Anglo-Soviet trade?

I replied that the Soviet Union was famous for its progressive attitude, but unfortunately in my case the people who had interviewed me had not shown themselves competent to judge the products and equipment my firms were offering. I therefore proposed that instead of taking my brochures and catalogues to the Ministry I should be allowed to bring to Moscow a delegation of technical specialists from the eight main companies I represented if Moscow in turn would provide Soviet personnel of a similar calibre. Direct discussions would then be possible without going through the normal administrative channels.

Was I in a position to arrange this? asked Bodenikov.

Certainly.

And how soon?

Before the end of the year, I said. This again was prophecy, since I had never mentioned a delegation to any of my firms.

Bodenikov looked pleased. Mineral drinks were passed round. Then Bodenikov went out and returned with a hearty female bearing coffee and vodka. There was informality at the green baize, and I was able to study the cast. Bodenikov himself was short and gross. Nylon shirt, Western tie, suit that appeared to have been slept in, crumpled hair, dirty fingernails, nicotine fingers, hands like a coal-miner, rough red face covered with blackheads, needed a shave. The next two men down the table were of the same ilk with variations, but the third man was different.

He had a very straight back and did not wriggle or slouch. He sat quite still, his pale firm hands resting on the cloth. His nails were manicured. He wore a soft silk shirt and a plain black tie. His suit was immaculate. Sunlight filtering through the uncleaned windows showed up his glossy reddish hair and deep-set eyes. His nose was broad-based and his mouth full-lipped and strong. A powerful imaginative face. His name was Colonel Oleg Penkovsky.

While the vodka was being served I took mental notes of all the others, but Penkovsky was the easiest to remember.

The meeting broke up and Bodenikov said he would report to the Committee. Two days later I was summoned again and brought up to the same room, this time on foot up the stairs because the lift had broken down. Arriving somewhat breathless, I was left alone with the two senior Committee men, Guishiani and Levin. Guishiani was the president, with direct access to Khrushchev. Levin was second in command. All smiles now. Guishiani personally approved my delegation and would welcome it himself. Vodka was brought. 'Soviet trade!' 'Anglo trade!' 'Anglo-Soviet trade!' 'The

Delegation!' The great men disappeared and the team I had met before filed in to discuss details. I asked whether visits to Soviet factories could be arranged. With pleasure. Colonel Penkovsky enquired about slide and film equipment. I noticed his rich deep voice. He appeared somewhat aloof and formal, but then he *had* missed the vodka. Later I was taken to lunch by Bodenikov, Levin and two other men. We ate at the National Hotel. Again the toasts to everything we could think of. When I emerged for a constitutional round Red Square my hopes for the delegation appeared unusually rosy.

Back in London I was closely cross-examined about the Committee in Moscow. Who was present? Their names? Their appearance? A pile of photographs was laid on the table. Some I recognised, some not. Who was this? And this? And this?

'That is Colonel Penkovsky.'

'Who did you say?'

'Oleg Penkovsky.'

A finger thrust towards the photograph: 'That is your man, Greville.'

Now my story grows. Now for the first time I knew what it was all about. Now I was told all that was known of Penkovsky: his cadetship at the Kiev Artillery School in 1939, his distinguished war career on the Ukrainian front, his appointment as Assistant Military Attaché in Ankara (1955), how he joined the Military Intelligence, the G.R.U., his course at the Dzerzhinsky Artillery Engineering Academy in Moscow (1959), and his present appointment with the Scientific Research Committee in 1960. This appointment gave the first real opportunity for our meeting. Now I understood the extraordinary prevision which had kept me in readiness through the waiting years, till now, when the opportunity had been so promptly taken. 'There is an organisation called the Scientific Research Committee,' echoed James's voice.

With haste I returned to the British firms and told them, truthfully this time, that Moscow was waiting to welcome them. The firms, eight in all, were at first reluctant, but at last, under my tempting hints of large contracts, agreeable. The delegation (in most cases two representatives from each firm) was arranged, and I went back to Moscow, five days ahead of their arrival, to find that the man chosen to supervise their welcome was Colonel Penkovsky.

My briefing was simple. I must make no overtures, give no hint that I expected anything from Penkovsky. And indeed there might be nothing to expect. But from our first moments together I had a feeling that London was right. It was as if for the first time I had been allowed to switch on a radio receiver. I was not yet tuned in, but I seemed to hear something. I noticed that when others were present at our discussions Penkovsky was withdrawn and correct but on the rare moments when we were alone he seemed to relax. He began to question me about my life in England, my home and background, gentle friendly questions. His eyes sometimes looked very straight into mine. He seemed—or was I wrong?—to be making some slow and careful estimation.

The day of the delegation's arrival dawned with thunder and rain. After lunch I went with Penkovsky and two other men to the airport, where we were told, with typical Soviet imprecision, that the plane *might* be diverted to another airfield on the other side of the city. Penkovsky sent his colleagues to the other airfield, while he and I waited for what he thought the more likely touchdown. But he was wrong, and after two and a half hours of his probing questions we heard that the British party was on its way by bus to the hotel. We drove back and waited for them. We waited a long time, and when they arrived their entry into Moscow was truly Soviet, for on the outskirts of Moscow the bus broke down and, in the usual absence of alternative transport, my fourteen weary directors, clad uniformly in splendid fur hats and long greatcoats from Moss Brothers, reached the hotel by pushing their own bus. If they had left the bus and walked they had been afraid they might never see their luggage again.

It was the beginning but not the end of their troubles. That evening, when they had bathed and chai.ged, I took them to a restaurant where a long table was waiting loaded with caviare, fish, salami and vodka. This splendid repast was only possible because Penkovsky had taken me to the restaurant that morning to arrange it. The directors, still grumbling about the bus, were only mildly appreciative. Next evening, after an initial welcome by Guishiani and an exhausting day of sightseeing, they again dined well without knowing their luck. On the third evening, after a long day of sightseeing, my party were feeling very chirpy. When I apologised for not having had time to arrange their dinner the general reaction was that I had been trying to steal a little credit. 'Never mind the arrangements, old boy. This town seems okay. Vive Moscow,' and so on.

'Perhaps you would like to choose your restaurant?'

'Sure, leave it to us.'

The restaurant they chose was the Praga, one of the best in Moscow. When we got inside we were left standing for half an hour in the foyer. Then an empty table was spied and we moved towards it. The table was covered with broken crusts and dirty glasses. We sat down and for the next hour, in spite of much waving and hand-clapping, no waiter came near us. But my directors were men of the world. They had funny stories to pass the time. Someone grabbed a menu. The dishes had English translations but no one paid any attention to our cries. Cigarettes stifled our pangs for a while, then we became nauseous. The jokes and the banter became acid. One by one the directors rose and searched for a waiter, but no one succeeded. It was suggested we move to another restaurant, but I advised against it. If this was the best restaurant what might the others be like? 'I'm going to die,' announced the hungriest director, but no one cared. We were all going to die if we did not get some food. It was now, after nearly three hours, that a waiter passed behind our table bearing a tray of fish for someone else. But the director was beyond etiquette. He whipped a plate of cold fish from the tray, held the plate firmly down on the table, and started to shovel up the fish with his fingers. Those nearest reached greedily for what they could get. The waiter rushed to the end of the restaurant and came back with six others who clamoured offensively round the fish thieves. At last a waiter was found who spoke a little English. Apologies were grudgingly offered and surlily accepted. Our order was taken. It was a formality, since only fish was obtainable. Forty minutes later the dirty glasses were removed and the fish was served. But the wine we had asked for was finished.

Now our throats took up the suffering. We would all die of thirst. But suddenly a cadaverous director, red with rage at the fish bone stuck between his front teeth, leapt up with the cry, 'My God, there's some beer over there!' On the far side of the restaurant was a line of frigidaires (proudly displayed to full view) with beer bottles on top. In moments there were fifteen bottles on our table, but no opener. Forks and pen-knives failed and there was talk of smashing the bottle necks against the table leg when our hero saw a waiter opening a bottle at the next table. The opener was seized, the waiter clung on, there was a tug-of-war and another convergence of wrathful Russians. We got our beer, but it was past midnight when we tottered out into the freezing street.

From now on I was allowed to bespeak our dinners.

Officially the visit of the delegation was a fair success. The lectures were well attended, our opposite numbers showed a genuine interest in British products, and some of our delegates were even permitted to visit factories in Moscow. These were mostly unimportant factories, whose inspection would reveal no secrets. This was Soviet policy. Other visitors were not so lucky. The factories they would have liked to see were outside Moscow, in some cases hundreds of miles away, and here the Russian genius for delay showed itself in full bloom.

The British delegates would, of course, be welcome at the factories, but varied and ingenious were the excuses for keeping them away. For instance, the case of a man I will call Douglas and the factory in the Urals.

Douglas was director of a company making machine tools. He was a family man with seven children, and he wanted to be home for Christmas. He was a sad stubborn Yorkshireman near the age of retirement.

The Urals factory, explained our liaison officer, was one of the most modern in the Soviet Union. Douglas smiled. Unfortunately the railway track had been damaged by frost. Trains were taking up to seven days to get there. Douglas didn't care. He was used to continental travel.

The new hotel, which was to have been finished last month, had also been delayed by the frost. There would only be second-class accommodation. Douglas was a Desert Rat. He did not mind roughing it.

It was most regrettable, but a telegram had been received only yesterday that some of the factory plant was out of service. Douglas shrugged. He would see what there was to see.

'In that case we shall be delighted to show you our machine-tool products in the Urals.'

'That is what I have come for,' said Douglas.

'There is only one other point. It would be unfair, perhaps, not to mention it.' The liaison officer paused. 'There have been a few cases of plague reported in the area. Two weeks ago there were seven deaths. Last week there were twenty-five. By now the epidemic is almost certainly under control.'

There was a long silence. We all looked at Douglas. He had often told us that when you have been a Desert Rat you have seen the lot. But Douglas, Rat that he was, did not fancy his chances with the plague. He mumbled that maybe he would see the Urals factory next time.

It is difficult to describe mounting tension, but I certainly felt the tension that mounted gradually in Penkovsky as the days passed. I attended the morning lectures and even de-livered one myself, but in the afternoons, when the delegates were away to factories and exhibitions, I had little to do. Penkovsky had organised the visit with immense thorough-ness, but he still seemed anxious for discussion. 'There are just a few points,' he would say, but when we were walking through the streets of Moscow or sitting alone together in the vast art galleries, the points for discussion seemed to be for-gotten. There would be long silences, then a sudden smile and the offer of a cigarette. Standing before a coin case in the Kremlin Museum he pressed his hands on the glass and stared as if hypnotised at the medieval relics. I spoke but he did not answer. When I spoke again he started and seized my arm. 'Let's get out of here. It's so gloomy, I can't stand it. I want some fresh air.' And off we marched, across Red Square and up the hill past Lubyanka prison, with the pale sun low in the leaden sky, our breath, especially mine, panting out into the freezing air.

Instinctively we liked each other, but this itself was to him a barrier. As a senior Intelligence officer with the G.R.U., he was trained to be suspicious of sympathy. He told me later that he had many times been on the brink of speaking, but dared not. It had seemed too much of a coincidence that the head of the British delegation, the very man with whom he could so easily be alone, should appear friendly and ready to listen. So we continued our walks and our sightseeing, and I saw the yearning and hesitation in his clear eyes, and there was nothing I could say to help.

On the last evening he took me to the Ballet. They were dancing *Swan Lake* and *Les Sylphides*. Sitting in the huge theatre, heavy with gilt and festooned with the mighty chandeliers of Czarist days, I felt the enormous response of the Russian people to what they so dearly loved. The Russians understand ballet as the English understand soccer. It was like being at Wembley for the Cup Final, the warmth, the absorption, the taking of every point.

Afterwards, with the music still in our ears, we went to a café and there, at a corner table with our beer, he sighed, as if he had come to some final conclusion, and said:

'Well, Greville—it's about time we dropped the surnames, isn't it?'

'Sure. And it's "Oleg", I believe.'

'That's right. Or, better still, "Alex". Your "Oleg" doesn't sound so good.'

'Cheers, Alex,' I said. 'I hope we meet again.'

'So do I, very much.'

'In London, perhaps. Have you been to London?'

'No. I should like to.'

'It's not impossible, is it? I have been to your country. Why don't you come to mine? You could bring a return delegation perhaps.'

'Yes, I might do that. Why not? It's a wonderful idea.'

'Then suggest it to your people.'

'No!' He hesitated. 'No, Greville, it would be much better if the suggestion came from you. Will you do that?'

'Of course.'

We had been speaking in low voices, and I noticed that he kept his hand or his glass in front of his mouth when he had something important to say. It is part of an agent's training to give no opportunity, especially in a bar or restaurant, for a private conversation to be lip-read. An expert lip-reader could have told what we were saying from several tables away.

'Yes, I've heard about London,' he repeated. There was a catch in his voice, as if the thought was almost too much for him to bear. He licked his lower lip and raised his eyes to mine. I looked steadily back and waited. Then I saw his eyes flicker to the next table and his expression suddenly change. There had been a party of four. Now only one man was left. He had his eyes shut and was sitting very still with folded arms. There was no proof. We did not know then, and we never knew. But the threat was enough, and Alex said in a polite voice, 'Well, I hope your chaps feel that it has all been worth while,' and I said very well worth while, I was sure, and we walked back to my hotel, where he said good night.

Next morning, before I left Moscow, I went to the Committee for the last time and proposed that a return delegation should be sent by the Soviets to London. I was told that an immediate answer could not be given, but my proposal would be considered.

At the airport Alex was there to see me off, but we were never alone, and the last I saw of him was as I reached the top of the gangway and looked back, and Alex raised his hand and turned away.

I was baffled. I could not understand it. During the flight home I racked my brains for an explanation. I was certain that Alex had wanted to say something, had been on the brink not once but many times. There had been plenty of opportunities. So what had prevented him?

I learnt the explanation several weeks later in London.

One of the eldest members of our delegation had been surprised one evening when Colonel Penkovsky came to his room and asked him to take a package to the Foreign Office in London. The old man, unprepared and with a natural terror of the illicit, especially on Soviet soil, had refused.

So Alex had not quite trusted me. I could not blame him, but it meant another exasperating delay. It was not till the following April, 1961, that I finally broke through to him, and then by a situation of my own making.

Back in Moscow, to discuss the possibility of a return delegation of Russians to London, I found Alex still as friendly as before, and still as hesitant. But when he presented me with the list of Soviet representatives who had been chosen to visit England I found that we were back with the inexperienced and the unsuitable. I protested, but Alex assured me that the list had been drawn up by the Committee and would not be changed.

'But who is this, Alex? My firms do not deal with these products.'

'Never mind. Just accept it, Greville, please.'

'And this man, Professor Kazantsev. Who is he?'

'He is an expert in radar. He is very interested in your Jodrell Bank.'

'But I am not selling Jodrell Bank. And what about all these men—they are not even experts. They are administrators, minor officials.'

We were walking across Red Square and the snow blew in our faces.

'But I shall be coming as head of the delegation, Greville.'

'I know that. But with all respect, it is not enough. I want the top technical advisers or no one. If I don't get them I shall complain to the Committee.'

'No, no, Greville, you mustn't do that. It would mean that the delegation was cancelled.'

Here suddenly I saw my chance. I said severely:

'I'm sorry, Alex, but I have to insist. I would like to show you London, but not if it means wrecking the whole purpose of the visit. My companies want experts.'

Then Alex clapped his hands together and cried:

'But it is not the delegation that matters. It is I who must come to London, and it is not for pleasure. I have things to tell you, so many things. I have got to come, I have *got* to.'

I asked him: 'Why, Alex? Why is it so important?'

In the whirling snow, where even the Soviets could not hang a microphone, he told me, quickly and gaspingly, all I needed to hear.

That night at my hotel he gave me a bulky package. 'Open it, Greville, see for yourself.' Inside was a complete dossier of himself and a film of Soviet military documents and papers which I saw would convince London ten times over. I did not tell him that I knew he had tried before, with the wrong man. There was no sense in looking over our shoulders. Alex trusted me now, which was all that mattered.

It was freezing at the airport next morning, so cold that the two uniformed and armed officials, instead of standing at the bottom of the gangway, took up positions in the plane itself. There were only three other passengers, and with the long envelope under my coat I showed my boarding ticket and was waved through to choose my seat.

Quickly I went as far aft as I dared, hid the envelope under some rugs on the luggage rack, and sat down a few places further for'ard. The other passengers took their seats, and through the window I could see Alex on the tarmac. We were all set to take off, but we did not move. A jeep arrived, and officers got out. Three appeared at the doorway of the aircraft. There were whisperings with the crew, and comings and goings on the tarmac. Twenty minutes since take-off time. Half an hour. I dared not appear too observant. I stared at my paper and waited, and thought about the envelope under the rugs, and waited. At last, thirty-five minutes late, we took off. I did not know what the fuss had been about, but evidently it had not been about me and my envelope.

As we taxied away I saw the straight figure of Alex wrapped in his greatcoat. He waved both hands, as if to erase the chilling moments we had shared. We were to share many others, but these were the first.

From now on it was not one against all, but two against the rest. It was a big difference.

# 2

# Lubyanka

## I

YOU *scrofulous nit. Stop scratching. Your fingernail is filthy. It does not help wiping your nail on your trousers because your trousers also are filthy. Unpressed. How did you ever get to be a general? Maybe you howled everyone down like you're trying to howl me down. You shouted and yelled and your red neck bulged over the collar, and they thought we must make him a general else he'll blow up. Some general! Big epaulettes indeed and plenty of medal ribbons. But what about a little shoe polish? It's unimportant? Okay, so you beat the German army. I grant that. You did it with manpower and a considerable amount of British equipment. And you did it with generals like Timoshenko.*

*You are no Timoshenko, General. You are a fat-bellied bleary-eyed bastard. And moreover, General, the war is finished. Your enemy now is not an army, it is a man, a man from Shropshire to be exact, and you don't want to kill him, you want to make him talk, you want to break down his resistance, and to do that you should try to impress him, you really should, and one way to begin would be to dazzle him with a display of super military efficiency. Shiny buttons, gleaming jackboots. Hitler understood that. Thank God it is not the Germans who are interrogating me. I would find it hard to resist the Teutonic splendour, whereas I find it easy*

*to resist the Soviet slovenliness. The dirty peeling brown
paint, the worn carpet, the windows smeared with birdshit.
It's a slum, General, and you are a slum child. I despise you.*

These are my thoughts while the General is speaking, but
they are not my feelings, I must make this clear. This is my
head talking and not my stomach. My stomach, if that is
where fear operates, is afraid. Whatever I tell about my life
in Soviet prisons you must imagine me always in a state of
apprehension, and sometimes just plain scared. I am in the
power of these animals like a child among gorillas. If I let my
stomach dictate I shall lose. To win, in any sense, I must find
a behaviour. So when I am alone in my cell, I clean it, and
when I am with the gorillas I answer back.

I cannot speak for the moment because the General is
speaking, so I think my thoughts, hearing the loud Russian
words which I do not understand.

We are in the interrogation room. Beside the General at
a big desk sits a lieutenant-colonel and beside me sits an
interpreter. We are at a small table and I have no doubt that
a microphone is passing all my remarks on tape.

It is a filthy room and my interrogators are a couple of
slovenly hulks. Thus far my thought is correct. Correct but
incomplete, for these hulks can do to me whatever they wish.
There is nothing they cannot do. But I do not think about
this. There is no need to depress myself. That will be done
for me. During these first forty-eight hours it is necessary to
hold them at bay, to give myself time to adjust. London had
warned me many times of these first forty-eight hours.

In the end I shall have to admit certain things, but it is
important that it shall be I and not the General who chooses
what shall be admitted and when. The General must be made
to believe that he is slowly extracting from me all I have to
tell. Some things he must never be allowed to extract, but he
must believe he is successful. To produce this effect will need
from me much delicate contrivance, so for the moment, while

the shock of capture is still working itself out and I am liable to make a mistake, I must avoid any positive statement about anything.

When the General has finished, the interpreter says quietly: 'How much were you paid for your espionage activities?'

'I am not a spy. I am a businessman.'

The interpreter repeats this in Russian. He is a soft, sad man. He is not exactly on my side, but he is not against me. The General's neck swells a little. He turns and mutters to the Lieutenant-Colonel, a pock-faced character with very black bright eyes. I must watch out for the Lieutenant-Colonel.

The interpreter says:

'You are in our power. You will never escape. We can keep you here for ever. We can shoot you if we wish.'

I reply as politely as I can:

'I quite understand that.'

'So it will save much time if you tell us the truth. We know everything about you.'

'In that case, with great respect, what is the point of my telling you what you already know?'

'Insolence will only make things bad for you.'

'Please allow me to put it another way. If you know everything about me you will know that I am a businessman who has come many times to your country in the interests of mutual trade.'

The General scratches his neck. He is lounging at the desk. He pushes a box of cigarettes towards me and I take one and the interpreter lights it for me and the Lieutenant-Colonel frowns. The General fiddles with a sheaf of type-written papers and breathes deeply as if trying to calm himself.

Then he says:

'Many times you visited the British Embassy in Moscow.

We have films of every occasion. Why did you go there?'

'Because it is a social centre. It is our club.'

'It is full of British spies.'

'I would suggest the General is mistaken.'

The interpreter does not like this but he repeats it impassively. The General thumps the desk and shouts and the interpreter says:

'Don't lie! You took material from the traitor Penkovsky. We know that. It is recorded in our films.'

'If the General would be kind enough to allow me to see these films I will endeavour to explain anything that may appear on them.'

'Don't tell me what to do! You will be shown what we choose to show you. Insolence from you will only bring punishment.'

'I have no intention of being insolent. I merely wish to help the General clear up any obscurities that may have appeared on the films.'

I have given only the outline of the conversation because the General tended to repeat himself and in each case I gave the same reply. Sometimes the General shouted, sometimes he talked through gritted teeth, sometimes he had long confabulations with the Lieutenant-Colonel before addressing me, but whatever noise and pantomime had gone on the interpreter always passed it on to me in a gentle even voice.

So far things have gone quite smoothly, but now I am bored. It is not all that funny to listen to the General shouting and the interpreter whispering. I want to freshen things up a little. My spasm of contempt for the dirty room has abated for the moment. Contempt is an emotion, and you can't keep up a violent emotion all the time. I am searching, you understand, for some attitude or policy which will help me, especially during the first dangerous period of shock, to deal with these blustering animals. Training has taught me to confuse my interrogators, so now I decided to begin. This policy of CONFUSION is to give me many moments of delight and satisfaction throughout my whole imprisonment, even towards the end when I am starved and beaten and do not care whether I live or die. Confusion to the Soviets! I hear the interpreter say:

'Let us stop all these stupid lies. Please give me a simple account of your activities.'

To which I reply:

'The principle is surely well known. It is electrical.'

The interpreter looks puzzled, but I open my eyes wide and nod sharply at him, and he, trained as he is to pass on exactly what he hears, repeats it to the General. They gabble for a few seconds, with the Lieutenant-Colonel chipping in, and then the interpreter says:

'We know that you are an electrical engineer. What we wish to hear is about your activities in the Soviet Union.'

I answer: 'I do not always bring these specimens to the Soviet Union. It depends which company I am representing. It would be difficult to explain the details unless I were allowed some paper.'

I talk like this because I am pretending that when the interpreter tried to say the word 'activities' he in fact said 'activators'. I do not quite know what an 'activator' might be, but I know that an 'actuator' is a solenoid-piston mechanism for transmitting motion, for instance to the flaps in the wing of an aircraft. So I am going to answer their questions as if the interpreter has said 'activator', when I know that he really meant 'actuator', and I foresee that when it comes to explaining to the General (through the interpreter) that the interpreter is guilty of a certain ignorance of the English language the poor interpreter will be in for a hot time. I am sorry. I like the interpreter, but I am afraid he must submit to being a pawn in the great and important game of confusion.

When I ask for paper, the General gives a snort and thrusts

On the steps of the Bolshoi Theatre—Greville Wynne (*far right*) with the British trade delegation.

The author's mobile trade exhibition in Bucharest. The mini-car in front was also carried in the trailer, in which Greville Wynne hoped to smuggle Penkovsky out of Russia.

The author with Levin and Guishiani of the Scientific Research
Committee in Moscow.

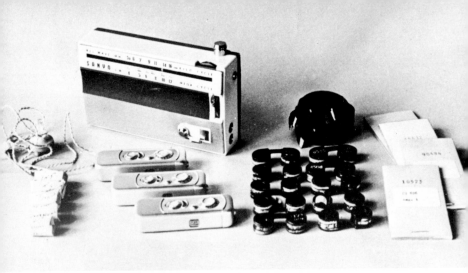

Transistor radio set, Minox cameras, cassettes and code books. This espionage equipment, alleged to have been used by Penkovsky and taken into Moscow by Wynne, was produced at the trial.

Penkovsky in the uniform of a lieutenant-colonel of the Red Army.

out some sheets of paper and a pencil, and growls something, and the interpreter says:

'I am pleased to hear you have come to your senses at last.'

I pick up the pencil and very carefully, watched by three pairs of eyes, I draw a small rectangle which I slowly black in, and from the rectangle a piston poking out, and at the end of the piston a rather inferior drawing of an aircraft flap. I push the drawing towards the General, and the General stares at it and goes crimson and yells, and the interpreter whispers:

'What is it supposed to be?'

'I am sorry,' I say in my most charming voice. 'I am not very good at free-hand drawing. It would be better if I were allowed some instruments. Then I could get the scale quite accurate.'

At this the General really starts bawling. I can see from the way his eyes dart from me to the interpreter that he is in doubt where the confusion lies. The General half thinks I may be making a fool of him, but this he cannot quite believe because I am his prisoner, and prisoners of the Russians simply do not indulge in humour with their interrogators. So perhaps it is something to do with the interpreter. But this is even less probable, and while the General is raving, the Lieutenant-Colonel grabs the paper and squints at it, and starts yelling at the General, and finally they both sink down in their chairs and the interpreter (whose face has visibly whitened during the commotion) says hoarsely:

'I don't know what all this nonsense is supposed to be. Will you now begin your confession?'

'But this is what the General asked for. That is a perfectly correct drawing of an actuator, a little out of scale, I admit.'

'Actuator?' says the interpreter.

'That is what you asked for.'

'I don't understand. What is an acci—actu—what was the word you used?'

'I was repeating the word *you* used. Actuator.'

'I did not use this word.'

'Pardon me, but this *is* my language.'

'No, no—I do not know this word.'

During this whispered dialogue the General has been growing restless. Now he shouts so loud at the interpreter that I decide the moment has come for an explanation. It is hard luck on the interpreter, but he must learn to take the rough with the smooth. So I clap my hand on my head and cry:

'Ah, I believe I know what happened.' The interpreter looks at me with gratitude, and I say:

'What you really meant to say was "activities", but you got mixed up . . . forgive me, you know English really quite well, but our pronunciation is not always easy. So you said "activators"—which doesn't mean anything at all, and I naturally assumed that you meant to say "actuators"—which would seem quite sensible, as I happen to be an electrical engineer.'

The interpreter, who speaks almost perfect English, is dazed by all this. His pride is hurt. He stares at me helplessly, and I prompt:

'Please be good enough to explain to the General what I have said.'

'But I assure you . . .'

The General barks and I murmur:

'Tell him exactly what I said.'

I doubt if any of the three has the least idea what an actuator is, but the uproar that arises when the interpreter tries to explain something he does not understand to the General, who gradually perceives that the interpreter, besides speaking in riddles, is also guilty of misinterpretation, is such that in the end even the interpreter has to shout to make himself heard. After fully five minutes of deafening jabber the General seizes the cigarette box and bangs it on the table for silence. He has a look on his face which I do not like at all, so I say quietly:

'I am extremely sorry if anything I have said may have led to confusion. I have been doing my best to answer the General's questions truthfully, and when this word "actuator" was used—through a pure misunderstanding, of course —I naturally thought the General was referring to my profession which, as the General knows, is that of an electrical engineer.'

The General listens to the translation and drums his fingers on the desk. He looks different now. Still badly dressed, but confident and brutal. I find it difficult to make light of the General when he looks like this. I reach towards the cigarette box, but the General snaps the lid and pushes the box out of my reach. He says via the interpreter:

'Well, Mr. Veen, we have not made a very good beginning. But never mind. We have plenty of time. We can take away your food, which will make you weak, so that you will not feel so cocky. We can take away your sleep. And many other things. Think about these things, Mr. Veen. You will be kept in solitary confinement until you make a full written confession. And just to start with, you will have no cigarettes for one week.'

I can find nothing funny in these words, nothing that can be twisted or made light of. The General means exactly what he says. My stomach is flooding with fear, but I am determined to make some reply. My voice sounds strange:

'All this is preposterous. I demand to see the British Ambassador.'

The interpreter repeats this and there is a silence. Slowly the General reaches for the cigarette box. He offers it first to the Lieutenant-Colonel, then to the interpreter and then to himself. When the cigarettes are lit, the blue smoke puffs out from the three faces, and nothing is said. The interpreter looks at the floor, but the other two look at me. They do not move or frown, they just look. I watch the smoke drifting past the tatty curtains. On the wall hangs a large photograph of Lenin, God of the Soviets. Lenin looks at me with his cold eyes. He says nothing. Why should he? I have asked a question and I am getting my answer. The silence is my answer, eloquent and complete.

The General presses a bell and a soldier appears and I am taken back to the lift and down, down, down to my cell.

That is the end of my first interrogation.

I am beginning to have a macabre affection for my cell. It is hardly comfortable, I must admit that. The bed has no springs, it is made of iron slats and it is too heavy to move. The mattress is hard and there is only one pillow and one blanket. A table, a stool, and one shelf on the wall. On the shelf is my tin mug and my metal spoon. The metal is soft and if I broke it and used the jagged end to stab the guard, supposing the guard were kind enough to open his tunic and lay aside his gun, I doubt if I could do more than bruise him. James Bond, I suppose, would kill the guard and gnaw the spoon into a skeleton key and open the steel doors and ascend in the lift and scamper past a dozen armed guards and find an aeroplane at Moscow Airport, or maybe there would be a convenient duct leading out of the cell ceiling. But I am not James Bond. I must admit, at the risk of seeming irresolute, that escape from Lubyanka is not just unlikely or difficult, it is inconceivable, and I never at any time make any attempt to conceive it. I concentrate on improving my cell and on not becoming too cold. These are my objects.

I improve the cell by cleaning it. I am not allowed any paste or polish, but in the lavatories are torn pieces of *Pravda* which I dunk in the pan and bring back to wipe my floor and furniture with fanatical devotion. The problem of cold is more difficult. My prison uniform consists simply of a thin vest and pants and dirty dungarees and canvas boots without laces or socks. It is November in what proves to be the coldest winter Europe has known for years, and the heavily barred radiator is tepid.

For one hour a day I am allowed to exercise in the pen on the roof. As you come out of the lift on the flat roof of Lubyanka the first thing you see is the raised wooden platform where the guards stand with their tommy guns. To your left is a large exercise pen. This is for prisoners who can mix with other prisoners. It is not for me. I am pushed into one of several smaller pens, to the right. They are about twelve feet square, they have high walls topped with barbed wire and are open to the sky. For exercise I am given an old greatcoat. The previous wearer had bugs, but as it is a choice between bugs and freezing to death, I choose the bugs. For the first week or two the bugs rejoice on my rich Western-fed blood, but as the prison diet takes its effect, the bugs stop feeding and I presume they have starved to death. Poor bugs! So I huddle in my greatcoat and stamp the snow into a runway, and do knees-up and arms-bend, and trot round my pen in figures of eight. I find that to trot in simple circles, whether left-handed or right-handed, produces a dangerous sense of depression, but with figures of eight it is much better. This is a small point, but my life is composed of small points, of innumerable minute routines and practices which give me heart. I think that if the Russians had really studied all these fragments of daily behaviour with which I comforted myself, and had prevented them, I might have lost heart, and I need my heart, every scrap of it.

For the first few days I trot round in silence, and then I start feeling lonely for voices, so I shout out, 'Anyone speak English around here?' and a voice from another pen comes back with a strong European accent, ' 'Ooray', but before I can develop this conversation one of the guards on the platform yells at me and waves his gun. So I leave it a couple of days, and then I begin to sing, quietly at first, and then louder, in the hope of getting a song back from someone. The guards do not seem to mind this, though my singing voice is grim, very grim. In a hot bath I can sing as well as the next man, but up here in the freezing Soviet air I sound awful. I am a pain in the ear to myself, but I troll a few numbers from *South Pacific*, and then I insert the chorus of Rule Britannia. Perhaps this will bring a response from another prisoner. But there is no response. Maybe they are all too afraid or maybe they just do not recognise my Rule Britannia. Whichever it is I cannot blame them.

After my hour on the roof I am taken down to my cell. It is nice to get back, like coming home from the office. It is my nest, certainly a lousy nest, but the only one available. It is very cold and the bed is hard and I am not allowed to lie down in the daytime. The only decoration is a list of prison rules written on the wall in Russian which I do not understand.

I would like to learn some Russian but that is not allowed. The only dictionary I am allowed is the English Pocket Oxford dictionary. I have a pencil and on the blank page at the end I start a calender, which is a series of squared columns with crosses to mark the days. I draw three hundred and sixty-five squares and put a cross in the first square for November 2nd. Each day I put one cross. This (like everything else I do in my cell) is observed through the spy-hole, and I am visited by the deputy warden, an army captain. He is a typical service officer, weary and correct, and he explains through the interpreter that marking the dictionary is not allowed. After an hour's polite argument I convince him that the making of pencil crosses will not threaten the Soviet Union in any way at all, and I am solemnly given permission to carry on. It is essential to keep contact with the outside world by recording the days, but the empty squares, reaching away in their hundreds, depress me. Sometimes I have an insane wish to put in several crosses at once as if to make time pass more quickly, but this I resist.

I grow almost fond of my cell. When I am inside, no one bothers me very much. But as the long days pass, the privacy which I enjoy threatens to become loneliness, which I do not enjoy. So which is it to be, privacy or loneliness? For most aspects of imprisonment and interrogation I had, as I shall explain later, been trained in England. But to prepare me for the long slow passage of confinement it would have been necessary to shut me up alone for months on end, and this was not possible. Even London, who overlook nothing, could not afford such a length of time. I had been warned, but no warning could fully prepare me for the reality when it came.

The worst part of loneliness is the beginning. Strange thoughts appear and your sense of value begins to wobble. What is important and what is unimportant get mixed up. For instance, the cold and the lack of nourishment and the difficulty of sleeping under a bright wall-light on an iron bed with a blanket which will cover either my feet or my shoulders but not both at once. These things, which are clearly of much importance, do not bother me. I am aware of them and I do not enjoy them, but I deal with them as best as I can and they do not occupy my mind. Instead I find myself occupied with something of no real importance whatever—the colour of the cell walls. The floor is made of red composition, and the ceiling, and the top part of the walls are whitewashed. But from floor level up to about four feet the walls are eau-de-Nil. The radiator, the bed, the stool, the table and the shelf are all eau-de-Nil.

Green is supposed to be a restful colour but this eau-de-Nil annoys me. At first I merely dislike it, then I start to hate it and think about it at nights when I am shielding my eyes against the bright light and soon I am fixated against the eau-de-Nil with a loathing which, if I am not careful, will seriously threaten the security of my little nest.

Action is needed to deal with this problem. I can imagine the sarcasm in London's voice when he says to me: 'Well, Greville, you took everything they could throw at you, and then you suddenly went whacky over the colour of your walls.' This would not do at all. A solution must be found and I find it, oddly enough, in the torn pieces of *Pravda* which I am allowed for lavatory paper. So far I have only scrubbed my floor and furniture, but now I start on the walls. I rub the grime off the eau-de-Nil.

After days of rubbing I clean off every speck of dirt, till the eau-de-Nil, instead of being uniform and grimy, is now clean. It is also patchy. The eau-de-Nil had not been put on too cleverly and my rubbing has now given it a mottled appearance, which for some absurd reason pleases me and gives me a sense of victory. I stop worrying about the eau-de-Nil.

The eau-de-Nil incident had one unexpected result. My cell is one of twenty-eight arranged round the sides of a rectangular hall. There is a similar pattern above, with a steel net to prevent any suicidal dives by the upper prisoners. There is a heavy steel door in the hall and on the other side of this door are two armed guards. Everything this side of the door, the cells and wash places and lavatories, comprise an area of confinement from which there can be no escape. There are no other doors to the outer world, and the windows are all small and high and barred. The guards therefore are not armed. They are male and female and wear the same military uniform, badly tailored and soiled indeed, but still roughly symbolic of some kind of army. Once in ten days the men take me to the showers (a concrete room with a rusty rose poking from the ceiling and the water controlled by a guard outside who will sometimes, if I bang and shout long enough, make the water hotter or colder) and to the lavatories (dark smelly boxes with a spy-hole in the door and only a pit to crouch over), and the girls bring the food to my cell.

In their impassive Slav faces I see no hint of human contact. I certainly expect no favours. But one morning when I am rubbing the eau-de-Nil with my lump of *Pravda* the shutter clicks and the door opens and the fattest girl beckons me. She takes me to a water tap I have not met before and gives me a bucket, a whole bucket of water and a rag. The water is hot, which astounds me, but it does wonders to my floor and furniture. So I am grateful to Fatty and still more grateful that afternoon when at a strictly unorthodox hour she brings me a cup of tea, and two days later some extra meat. Later on one of the men catches the same idea and he too gives me food and the odd cigarette on the sly. The soldiers in Lubyanka are simply doing a job. Except for these two they are impassive and correct, but they never make things worse than the rules dictate. 'Not evil but misled.' How many hundreds of times have I heard Penkovsky say that about the Soviet people? It is only the rulers who are evil.

My interrogations continue, every morning and some afternoons. The Lieutenant-Colonel takes over. He is quieter than the General but more hostile. The General is not pleasant to me but he looks as if he would be capable of pleasantness, to his superiors or his mistress. But the Lieutenant-Colonel looks thoroughly incapable. He drones on for hours about how much he knows of my activities and why won't I be sensible and co-operate, and I keep repeating that I don't know what it is all about, and after a week of this I start to feel surprised that this mean-faced cold-eyed bastard is not exercising his powers to more effect. My cigarette ration has been restored, which may simply be because that was the order and he has forgotten to extend it. But the interrogations are getting nowhere and many times, from the sudden contraction of his eyes, I get the impression that he would enjoy being much tougher with me.

Then why isn't he?

One morning in the middle of interrogation I am taken in
the lift to a new floor and down a corridor to the hall and up
to the door of a cell. For a moment I think that this is going
to be my new cell, and then the Lieutenant-Colonel gives an
order and the guard puts his hand over my mouth and draws
back the spy-hole shutter and the Lieutenant-Colonel says:

'Look, Mr. Veen, and tell us if you recognise this man.'

I put my eye to the slit and there sitting on the metal bed
is Penkovsky.

His hands are between his knees and his head is hanging
low. His face is thin and hidden with straggly stubble, but it
is Penkovsky all right. No, not Penkovsky, the wreck of
Penkovsky. He is a terrible sight. He sits motionless with his
head down, like a bull after the lance-wound has weakened
him, when the red strength is pouring down his shoulders.
They have not bled Penkovsky but they have drained his
strength by starvation and lack of sleep. I am looking at the
remains of Penkovsky. I feel sick and wish he would move,
but he does not move.

Alex, what have they done to you?

I am taken back and the Lieutenant-Colonel says through
the interpreter:

'Well, Mr. Veen, now you have seen the traitor Penkovsky
and you must understand that he has told us everything—so
what is the point in being so obstinate yourself?'

'I am sure that he has told the truth, which is, as he knows
very well, that I have only visited the Soviet Union as a
businessman and in no other capacity.'

'And what about the packages and letters?'

He smiles, like a snake. 'We have films of you receiving
packages. Do not be foolish enough to deny this.'

Now here I have to think very fast. The policy, hammered
during my training, is never to deny what is definitely known
by the interrogators. Denial of known facts would destroy

the illusion that they are extracting the truth bit by bit. The arrangement between Alex and me was that if we ever were caught we would tell what we knew was known, but would stick firmly to the line that I was a businessman and nothing else. I am certain that whatever they have done to him he will have stuck to this, so now I say:

'It is true, as you say, that I was given some letters and so on, to deliver in London or Paris if I was passing through. I was told they were merely business letters or presents which might reach their destination more quickly if I took them. I never looked at them carefully, and have no idea what they may have contained.'

'Surely you remember some of the names and addresses on these letters?'

'I am afraid not. I was not in the least curious. I delivered them but I forget where.'

'I would have thought that a trained spy such as yourself would have automatically registered such things.'

I reply pleasantly: 'But I am not a trained spy.'

After another hour of this I am taken back to my cell and hardly have I got inside before the door is opened again and two guards bring in a second metal bed and another stool and a few minutes later they bring in George. He is a Russian prisoner, and the first thing I notice is his hands, which are bloated and discoloured. His body must once have been powerful but now it is bowed and slow-moving. He speaks good English, and when we exchange names he can say 'Greville' perfectly well but I cannot pronounce his long Russky appellation, so I call him George.

The question is, why has George been put in my cell? And the only possible answer is that George is here to pump me. He is not here because the Lieutenant-Colonel wishes me to have pleasant company. Not that George is exactly pleasant. His hands are horrible and his face has a trampled look and his eyes are watery and mean and he has body odour.

Still, he is matey enough, and soon admires the cleanliness of my eau-de-Nil, and I wait with interest for the pumping to begin, but, of course, the Lieutenant-Colonel is not this stupid. He has ordered George to play it slow. They must know that any trained agent would be aware of the pumping routine. But they are not certain whether I am an agent, not quite certain. So the idea must be that in spite of myself I shall one day start talking to George about myself. It will not matter much exactly what I say so long as it is something positive which can afterwards be taken up by the interrogators and sifted and re-examined and maybe it will contain some casual statement which reveals more than I intend. Interrogation is like psychoanalysis. If you talk long enough, for hundreds or, if necessary, thousands of hours, you are bound to say something significant. The Lieutenant-Colonel has so far not done too well with his interrogations, so he thinks that perhaps George will start things moving, will prise open a few doors in my obstinacy. In the meantime the right atmosphere must be achieved.

The food improves and we get bits of meat in the thin soup and some margarine and sometimes two pieces of sugar for the day instead of one. The deputy warden tells us we may order things from the shop and when I point out respectfully that I cannot do shopping without some of my money which has been confiscated he says I can have a small credit, and with this credit I buy cigarettes and margarine and extra bread.

Altogether it looks like being quite a ball so long as George remains in my cell. The interpreter visits us and brings draughts and chess and a list of books I may get from the prison library. William Shakespeare and Karl Marx and Charles Dickens and Jack London.

Now William is a big man, I know this. I am proud to have been born in a county so near to William's. We both came to London to work, which is another link, I suppose. But this, at the present time, is the end of my sympathy for William. To appreciate and hoist in this deluge of words and ideas you need, in my opinion, a lot of surplus energy. You need to be well fed and all your glands rampant. When I open the book at random and read: 'Night's candles are burnt out and jocund day walks tiptoe on the misty mountain tops', I do not, quite frankly, respond. The tips of my toes are so cold at night that I can hardly sleep, and, speaking from my own limited experience, I have never met a day that could walk. The best use I can imagine for William is the slogan which a friend in advertising once invented to help sell petrol: 'Ann Hathaway with Shakespeare and Shell hath a way with motorists.' I think that is very good.

And the same with Karl Marx. I am too occupied with survival to bother about social philosophy, and if this guy is, as I understand, responsible for the present Soviet system, then I am against him.

So it comes down to Dickens and Jack London, and of the two I prefer London. Dickens is either too funny or too sad. This Pickwick gang might as well be on another planet as far as I am now concerned, and when it comes to prisons I reckon that by the time I have finished I shall know more than Dickens. So I take Jack London because he tells about simple things like dogs and snow and women in language that does not make my belly ache.

For several days George and I play chess and draughts and talk about the food, and then one evening he tells me about his arrest. He was wandering about near the border, it seems, and he was dead drunk and climbed through the wire of some forbidden sector, and for this he was given fifteen years in a labour camp. The camp had barbed wire all round, then a space twenty yards wide, then another fence. In the belt between the two fences were savage half-starved dogs. The dogs were restricted by long wires running on horizontal poles, so that each dog covered a section of his own, but every inch of the space was covered by one dog or another, and no human being could have walked across the space. So it was necessary to tunnel, and although George's account of the tunnelling is somewhat enigmatical, I gather he and a pal dug themselves under both fences, and appeared one dark night out of the ground and into the snow where the temperature was about thirty degrees of frost. They had little food, and there was nothing for a hundred miles but more snow and frost, so they lasted only three days before they were picked up, and all they had achieved was a beating, two months' solitary confinement, and frostbite. This accounted for George's swollen cracked hands.

Well, this is all very touching and I see that George expects me to match his confidences with a few of my own, but instead I give him a little lecture on bodyline bowling which baffles both of us.

He takes this rebuff fairly well, but I can see him brooding, and two mornings later, while we are exercising together on the snowy roof, he tells me about his arrest. But this time it is a different story. We are trotting round abreast of each other in figures of eight and George suddenly begins:

'I do not know where they got you, Greville, but my own arrest took place in Odessa. I was on vacation there, and one day I was approached by an American and before I knew what was happening he was suggesting I did a little work for them—you know?—and I was foolish enough to accept a few drinks in his hotel and, of course, our people were watching us and I was arrested on charges of espionage.' George adds naively, 'I don't suppose your experience was anything similar?' and I say, 'Oh no, nothing of that sort.'

But at the word 'Odessa' there is a big clang in my mind, because I was in Odessa myself about five years ago, and it is clear that the Lieutenant-Colonel hopes that if I speak of Odessa, as I now must (since I am known beyond doubt to have been there), I shall say something indiscreet.

The truth was that early on, when I was being steered towards Penkovsky, I was given a separate assignment in Odessa to make contact with someone who was ultimately extracted from Russia and is now in the United States. I was given this assignment to test my ability before continuing with the more difficult and elaborate matter of linking with Penkovsky. Having made contact I was to arrange the moment of escape for the man whose name is no part of this story. In Odessa harbour was a ship which I was to board as a tourist travelling to Varna. The ship was supposed to sail at midnight, but this would be postponed, and I was to go on deck, in pretence of curiosity, and at the stern I would find some rails had been removed for loading, and I was to 'fall' overboard on to some sand, which would be waiting on the dockside, and yell at the top of my voice so that the dock guards would come running, and the man in question could make his escape on to another ship in another area of the docks.

All went well, and everything happened as I had been told until it came to going overboard. It was very dark, and I found the gap in the rails, but someone had erred on the location of the pile of sand and I landed on concrete and broke my thigh in two places. The yell I gave before I passed out was certainly no fake, and when I came to I was pleased to find myself surrounded by the ship's purser and a crowd of harbour police.

I was taken to Odessa hospital (where I found once again the warmth and friendliness of the ordinary people, the patients and their visitors who gave me food), and after visits from a top Moscow surgeon (flown especially down for me) my leg was put in a plaster cast and I was flown to Moscow and afterwards to London, where my thigh was mended with steel pins whose presence, now in the cold of Lubyanka, gives me much ache and stiffness.

Now the Lieutenant-Colonel knows about my leg but not

about my errand. He suspects that what at the time was accepted as a tourist episode may have had another significance, but he does not know. So it is easy for me to answer the panting George by saying:

'It is funny you should have been arrested in Odessa because I was there myself some years ago. I was in the Union on business, and as it was Easter I took a few days off and planned to go to Varna, but unfortunately I fell off the ship and broke my leg on the dockside and I must say that your hospital did a wonderful job for me. You have fine doctors in the Soviet Union, not so fine as in England, but still very good.'

Poor George. He tries hard to keep on the subject of my visit to Odessa, but all he gets is a callous account of the strip clubs in Soho. He listens with enforced politeness to my saucy tales and I can sense his frantic desire to get on with his allotted task. But in this he fails and a few days later he is withdrawn from the cell and a new treatment begins.

For some days my leg has been aching badly, and at nights the steel pins in the bone feel like needles of throbbing ice. My prison boots are also bad. They cramp my feet, and I complain to the deputy warden that I cannot be expected to co-operate in my interrogations if I am forced to hobble into the room like a crab, and to my surprise the deputy warden goes away and returns an hour later to say I may have not only my own shoes but a complete outfit of my civilian clothes, and at my next interrogation the Lieutenant-Colonel gives me what is almost a smile and says:

'Well, Mr. Veen, so you see we wish to be reasonable with you and to deal with this whole matter in a sensible and cultured manner.'

'Good. And I hope that the culture will include my being allowed to shave,' I answer, rubbing my stubble, 'because I find this mess rather offensive.'

'The razor would not be allowed, Mr. Veen. I am sure you understand that we would not wish you to perhaps cut yourself.'

'But I have an electric razor in my luggage.'

'The electric razor would be allowed.'

My razor has a lamp-socket adaptor, so here I am shaving myself in my cell, wearing my own clothes, and being taken daily for interrogations which become almost soporific in their monotony and lack of bluster. A tape recording is played to me and I hear the voices of Alex and myself. I recognise the conversation as having occurred in a restaurant. I am saying I have a letter for Alex and he is thanking me.

'Who was this letter from, Mr. Veen?'

'I am not sure, but I think it was from a business acquaintance in Paris.'

'But why should you smuggle letters from Paris?'

'Pardon me, but I was not smuggling. I brought the letter by hand because, as I think you will agree, the postal system in the Soviet Union is not one of the fastest in the world by any means.'

'You knew, didn't you, Mr. Veen, that smuggling letters is forbidden? It is quite clear from this sort of thing that you are a spy.'

'I do not see the connection. I was not aware that it is forbidden to bring mail by hand. In our Western democracies this is a common practice between friends. I was ignorant of this rule of yours, but that does not make me a spy.'

On and on, day after day, droning through the long hours, the Lieutenant-Colonel's metallic voice and the interpreter's gentle voice, and on the wall the silent Lenin, and all the time I am wondering what is the meaning of the civilian clothes and the razor and the comparative improvement in diet. Surely they do not imagine that some clothes and a few morsels of food will soften me into telling them what they wish to hear? The crosses in my calendar show me I have been in

Lubyanka for over six weeks, and apart from admitting a few facts which would not prove me even in a Soviet court-room to be a spy, I am still denying everything. No, there must be another reason, and the most likely is that the British Embassy, who are certain to have made a fuss, have forced them to grant a visit. If I am visited by an Embassy official I must appear in fair health and be able to tell him that I have not been too badly treated.

It seems one morning that I have calculated correctly, be-cause I am taken to a room where my luggage is brought and I am asked to choose my best suit, and an hour later this suit is given to me all brushed and pressed. My shoes are cleaned and I am given a tie, and, when I am dressed up, the warden and a guard (both in civilian clothes) take me to the adminis-trative block and I notice that all the guards we pass on the way are dressed as civilians. Is this in honour of my visitor? I am wondering whether it is someone I know from the Em-bassy when the warden stops outside a door and the inter-preter comes out and says:

'Mr. Veen, when you go in there you will be very pleased with whom you see, but, remember, if you speak badly about anything to do with the Soviet Union the meeting will be over.'

When I go into the room I see the Lieutenant-Colonel, now a civilian, and standing beside him I see not an Embassy official but my wife.

For a second I do not believe it. A strange shudder sweeps up my body and into my head. I wonder if I have gone mad. The interpreter's words prepared me for someone, but this is not someone, it is Sheila.

We embrace without speaking and I feel her shoulders through the cloth and her warmth against me and her cheek on mine. When we stand away she smiles and says, 'Hello, Grev,' and I can't say anything. I am shaking all over and I can only cry, not big tears, just small tears that hurt my eyes. Sheila is a good girl, she does not cry, though I can see she is very near to it. 'Well, here I am,' she says, 'and every-one sends their love, especially Andrew,' and by now I have collected myself and I ask whether Andrew got the racing car I sent him from Vienna, and she says the car set is fine. 'And look,' she says, 'I've brought you some things.'

There is a suitcase on the floor, and the Lieutenant-Colonel nods and the interpreter puts the case on the table and opens it. There are fur-lined boots and gloves and woolly underwear and two heavy pullovers and thick socks. Also many cigarettes and a bottle of whisky.

The Lieutenant-Colonel says we can have one hour to-gether and motions to us to sit down. He nods at all the articles from the case, except the bottle of whisky. He makes a joke about the whisky and the interpreter explains that per-haps Mrs. Veen had better take the whisky back with her be-cause it may be a cold journey and Sheila puts her hand in mine on the table and we link our fingers and press them one by one in our own special way. The feel of her hand and the sound of her voice are among the things I have not let myself think of in Lubyanka. Sometimes at night the thoughts come, and I would quickly begin some recitation or catalogue, but now I stop struggling and squeeze her hand, and turn so that I can see her face.

She tells me about Andrew and the house and all our Chel-sea friends and in her eyes I can see our home. She asks about my food and I say it is not bad, 'but not quite like home perhaps'.

'You wouldn't mind a goulash, I daresay?'

'I certainly would not.'

'I haven't done one lately.'

'Well, you won't forget how, will you?'

'Oh no, I can still remember.'

Her wrist watch tells me that half the hour has gone, and when she sees me looking at the watch she twists it round to the other side of her wrist, and gives a little smile and goes on talking.

With the interpreter listening there is no point in trying to be clever, to slip in remarks with a double meaning, and anyway I have nothing of that sort to tell her. I do not wish her to share Lubyanka.

We have only a few minutes left now and I want to hear about home and about Andrew. I feel the minutes going, and I know there are many things I shall wish I had asked, and I keep looking at her grey eyes and her snub nose, trying to fix them in my memory, and then, just when we are discussing what she can get Andrew for Christmas, the Lieutenant-Colonel makes a sign and the interpreter says:

'You may say goodbye to your wife. You must go now.'

As we stand up the warden comes in with a guard. My mind goes blank. Surely there is some way . . . But there is no way. Then Sheila puts her arms round my neck and kisses my lips quickly and pushes me gently towards the door, and I walk out without looking back at her.

We go to the cell and the guard brings the armful of clothes and I am shut in, alone.

It was impossible that she came, and now it is impossible that she is gone. I sit on the bed and I can still feel her lips. The emptiness is too big to describe.

I am empty even of tears.

For five days after Sheila's visit I am left alone without interrogation and these are bad days, the worst I have so far experienced. I say, so far. To have that intense warm hour, and then to have nothing but myself, no break in the twenty-four hours except a trot round the freezing roof-pen, no images but my own, no words from the Lieutenant-Colonel to break my thoughts. If you are starving in a cold dark street you cannot do worse for yourself than inhale at the open doors of a busy well-lit restaurant. Man, have pity on yourself. Your taste buds were doing their best not to bother you, but now you have roused them. You are going to suffer for that deep inhalation of home.

I still have the clothes and cigarettes, and my daily hour in the snow pen is almost a pleasure with my feet in the fur-lined boots and my woolly underwear and my hands buried in the cosy gloves. But these luxuries remind me of home, and I cannot snuggle my toes and fingers without thinking of Sheila; not too much thought, I must not allow this, but I cannot avoid a little.

The Russians have done this deliberately, and I hate them for it, and when I am taken for interrogation on the sixth day I am in a mean mood. I decide to be difficult with the Lieutenant-Colonel, to foul things up for him.

But the Lieutenant-Colonel is mean too this morning and he gets his foul in first. As soon as I enter the room and take out a packet of cigarettes he snatches them and yells:

'No smoking! This isn't a party any more! All that has finished! Now we are going to be serious!'

We are going to begin, it seems, with my first visit to Eastern Europe, to Poland in 1955. They know the date and the hotel I stayed in. So why did I go to Poland? Whom did I meet? Was this where I began my espionage activities?

I answer that I was in Poland on business and I have never been a spy.

'Very well, Mr. Veen. So you are still asleep. But now you are going to wake up out of your dreams. You will go back to your cell and you will be given paper, and you will write down for us a full and accurate confession and you will not come out of your cell until you have done this.'

Hardly am I back in the cell when a ream of coarse paper is brought in—and all my possessions are taken out. My clothes, shoes, books, cigarettes, razor, cardigans, boots, gloves. Everything. I am back in the itchy thin uniform and canvas boots, and my only luxuries are the scraps of *Pravda* which I slip next to my chest under the vest or wrap round my feet at night where the blanket does not reach.

Next morning I wait for my hour on the roof. My circulation badly needs this hour. But I do not get it. For the next three weeks I stay in the cell. The only possession I am allowed to keep is the Oxford dictionary. I say I must have the dictionary to do my writing.

*You bastards, to hell with you. Do you suppose in your dirty minds that I will set even one word on paper? And you cannot force me. You can mutilate me to death, but that will not achieve the handwriting, and it is the handwriting you need. My signature on some typed concoction would not be enough. I would say afterwards that it was given under duress. You want the confession to show the world, or at least to have in reserve, should the world be sceptical. You need the handwriting like bankers need gold to back their print. And you will never get it.*

I will not write, but I will not sit doing nothing. It is almost too cold to hold the pencil, and my food, my only fuel for warmth, has been disimproved. The black bread is slimy. One mug of weak tea per day and a lump and a half of sugar. One bowl of Soviet porridge, tasteless gruel, the half-cooked grains mushed in tepid water.

Holding the pencil is not easy, but I have plenty of time, and slowly, with many scrumplings-up because I have no rubber, I design a splendid kitchen for my Chelsea home. I break my pencil and use one half as a straight-edge. I do the ground plan, then each wall in elevation. I have a Moffat electric cooker and a canopy and a Vent-Axia smell extractor. I have a treble sink and a giant fridge and a Wastemaster and a washing-up machine and a Kenwood mixer and an electric carving knife. I have everything. I do a full wiring diagram and a very cunning system of cupboards and shelves. It is probably the most beautiful kitchen in the world. I am very proud of it. I show it to all my friends. Some meal we shall have from this kitchen, some goulash!

When I am on the wiring diagram I see from my crosses that it is Christmas Eve, so I devote this day to making myself Christmas cards. It is doubtful if I shall receive a card from the Lieutenant-Colonel, but by bedtime I have cards from Sheila and Andrew and all my friends. Before I go to sleep I lay out the cards which are sheets of wavy paper. I have nothing to make them stick on the walls. My sellotape has been taken away. So I lay the sheets on the table and on the stool and beside my bed, and the cards from home I bend across the top and hang from my shelf with the mug and spoon as weights. When my breakfast comes I eat a third of the black bread and put the half-lump of sugar in my tea, and wish myself a Merry Christmas. I don't say Happy, I say Merry.

It is a short Merry Christmas because the guard notices the array of cards, and less than an hour later he comes back and takes them away. It tickles me that he could not act on his own initiative. He has to ask someone. In the Soviet Union everyone has to ask someone before they act. That is why Penkovsky lasted as long as he did, for months after he was first under suspicion—because he was so high up himself that it took months for the queries to go step by step up the ladder till they found someone high enough to give an order. It had to be step by step. You can't start jumping rungs in the Soviet Union.

So now I return to my kitchen, and I wonder how Alex is doing and whether he remembers it is Christmas. I wonder very much how Alex is coping.

All the time I have been drawing and designing I have been observed through the spy-hole, and I am aware that my popularity is slumping badly, because when the deputy warden visits me he no longer has any hint of friendliness in his voice. I calculate that if I had started writing, they would soon have had me back for interrogation. They can see I am only drawing and they are thinking that presently I will come to my senses and start a confession. So let them wait. They leave me three weeks, by which time I have finished my kitchen and a couple of dozen cars, expensive models far superior to the Soviet Moskovich.

At the end of three weeks the Soviet patience breaks and suddenly one morning the deputy warden rushes into my cell! with two guards. My drawings are swept together and I am hustled up to the interrogation room. The General grabs the drawings, skims through them, and says:

'What is all this, Mr. Veen?' and before I can reply, he yells: 'Stand up! Attention! Now—what is this nonsense here?' He waves the paper.

'That is a new kitchen for my home.'

'And this?'

'That is a Rolls-Royce. You do not see many in Moscow. It is the best automobile in the world.'

'And this and this and this?'

I explain the diagrams till the General says:

'That is enough,' and has a hurried gabble with the Lieutenant-Colonel, and then shouts:

'Very well, Mr. Veen. Evidently you are refusing to write your confession because you do not believe that we already know all about you. So we shall have to prove it to you. We shall do that tomorrow. Wait till tomorrow, and see what we have in store for you.'

I am not impressed by this bogey talk. Today is enough without worrying about tomorrow. So it is a surprise next morning when I am taken to a new and larger interrogation room which is crawling with generals and civilians who are probably from the K.G.B.

They are seated round the walls, and huddled on a chair at the far end of the room is the bowed figure of Alex Penkovsky. He has his back to me, but when he hears the scuffle on my entrance he turns and jumps up from the chair and cries:

'Greville! Oh, Greville—I am sorry!'

He is a terrible sight, almost an apparition. I only see his sunken staring eyes for a moment, because the guards grab him and slap him down again facing away from me. I have no chance to say a word directly to Alex because the General yells at me to keep silence unless I am addressed. Between Alex and me there is the length of the room, and unfortunately a bulky guard is standing behind Alex so that I can see only his legs and feet. Unfortunately, because I am waiting for a signal from Alex.

The signal had been devised by London, who overlook nothing. London foresaw that if this happened, if we were both caught and confronted with each other, it would be essential for me to know whether Alex had been able, under interrogation, to keep to the prepared story of me as an innocent or largely innocent businessman. So the signal, if we met standing up, was for Alex to place the heel of his left foot against the instep of his right, making an angle. If he was seated he was to rub the back of his neck with both hands in a natural gesture of stiffness.

In the moment of crying my name Alex had no time for signals. From his shocked cry and the look on his face I guessed that he had not been told of my capture. I can imagine what he is thinking now, as he sits with his back to me. I wish the guard would move aside.

Now the interpreter begins:

'Mr. Veen, how much money did you give the traitor Penkovsky?'

'I gave him no money.'

'We know you gave him money in return for his activities as a spy.'

'I gave him no money.'

'And how much did he give you?'

'None.'

'The prisoner Penkovsky has stated that friends of his in London gave him four thousand roubles to send back luxuries from the Soviet Union, and that he gave some of this money to you to buy presents for your wife.'

That was not true. Alex may have had some reason for saying this, but I cannot guess the reason. At such moments my instructions are to keep to the truth. To be caught out in small lies will make it harder for me to get away with the big lies. So now I say:

'I took home presents from time to time, but they were not bought with money from Penkovsky, because he never gave me money.'

Now Alex says something. He speaks in Russian (by order, I suppose) and the interpreter says:

'The prisoner Penkovsky asks, does Mr. Veen remember the fur coat?'

This must mean that Alex has told them how he and I went to a fur shop one day and looked at the foxes and sables and asked the prices. So I say I remember the fur shop.

'Where you bought a coat for your wife?'

'No, that is not correct. I asked the prices but I bought nothing.'

'The prisoner Penkosvky states that you bought a coat.'

Again I am out of my depth. I do not know whether Alex really said this, and, if so, why. So I say that it is true I told him I was going to buy a coat, but afterwards changed my mind.

'And the other packages and presents you took to London for Penkovsky?'

'It is true I took various parcels.'

'What was in them?'

'I do not know. They were sealed. I do not look inside other people's parcels.'

Some of those parcels were sealed all right! They contained thousands of feet of undeveloped microfilm of the topmost military and political secrets of the Soviet Union.

Now here the questions are getting dangerous. For Alex more than for me. If I am asked details of these parcels, and I give answers different from the answers Alex has been giving to his interrogators they may use my contradictions to make things bad for him.

But Alex rescues with a diversion:

'The prisoner Penkovsky asks whether you recall the candelabra?'

'Yes, I do.'

'These were given to you to take as a present from Penkovsky to someone he knew in London?'

'That is so.'

'But how did you know they were candelabra? You have said that you never knew what was in the parcels.'

'I was speaking in general terms. Candelabra are not easy to pack, and the Soviet wrapping paper is not of the highest quality. The ends of the candelabra were poking through the wrapping.'

On and on go the questions. When? Where? How big? What time of the year? How many? How often? And still I am not sure how much they have got out of Alex, and, above all, whether he has been strong enough to keep back the truth about me. He has already been under great pressure, how great, how terrible, I can only guess. And still the guard stands blocking my view of the signal. Or perhaps the signal is not coming, because Alex has cracked. For this I would never blame him. There is a limit to any endurance.

I am waiting and wondering and answering the questions as best I can when suddenly the General gives an order which is not translated, and two guards go to Alex's side, and the guard standing between us moves to open the door.

Alex is rising from the chair. He cannot turn round, but as he rises he puts his hands behind his neck, and bends his head as if it is stiff, and rubs the back of his neck with his fingers.

Then he is marched out, and I feel ashamed for even considering it is a possibility that he might have cracked. He has kept fast to the story. He has told nothing about me except that I was an ignorant messenger. Now that I know this I shall know how to face the long interrogations ahead. I shall take strength from the signal of those rubbing fingers.

For weeks afterwards this sight of the shrunken drooping Alex trudging between two massive guards to be reincarcerated in the inescapable cell, stared at by a score of brutal faces, the power-masters of two hundred million subjects, this image of the child with a lion's heart, the prisoner of lions with souls of vermin, burns in my mind like a sun-circle on closed eyelids, the image of freedom among a vast slavery.

## II

When Alex strode from Customs into the main hall of London Airport in April 1961 he was carrying two heavy suitcases as if they were matchboxes. He could only greet me formally, since he had six colleagues to introduce, but when we reached the hotel at Marble Arch, and the others were taken up to their rooms, he seized me in a bear hug in the middle of the foyer, held me away with his hands gripping my shoulders, and cried, 'I can't believe it, Greville, I just can't believe it!'

The Russian delegates were put two to a room, except Alex, who had a single. This was important, for at nights, when his official work was done, he had to be whisked away to a nearby apartment block where his real work began.

Here one floor had been taken over by British Intelligence. Most of the rooms were filled with unsuspecting civil servants who never knew what went on behind the few remaining doors. There were two or three offices, a conference room, and (the heart of the matter) an operations centre. Here, in place of the prim bedroom furniture, were installed typewriters, tape-recorders, coding machines, radio equipment, a private line to Washington, and a projector for slides and films. Stenographers, typists and interpreters in case of technical language difficulties. A doctor with stethoscope, syringe and pep pills to keep Alex awake and alert; during his whole stay in London he never had more than three hours' sleep a night. And relays of British and American Intelligence officers to question, question, question.

The material I had brought in advance had astounded London, who to their credit saw that this was no time for parochialism. The Americans were given full access to the priceless information, and late that first night Alex was received in the conference room by the men who had so eagerly awaited him.

It was not considered necessary for me to be present, so when Alex came into the room he found a crowd of faces he had never seen before. Intelligence chiefs, Service chiefs, and one higher than they, a man whose name is among the most famous in the country. They began their greetings, but Alex, looking round the room, said: 'Where is Greville Wynne?' and in spite of reassurances, refused to speak to anyone till I had come from Chelsea.

Over-caution, perhaps, but I understood it so well. Alex had made up his mind that he could trust me, and in the nervy world of espionage a feeling of trust is the rarest experience of all. Even rarer for Alex than for me. Since the day of my first recruitment, to whatever moments of isolation and danger I had been brought, there were always men to whom I could turn, to whom I could talk with absolute confidence. But Alex had for years, till I broke through to him, moved quite alone. It was true now, tonight, that I had told him the number of the room and the name and appearance of the man who would open the door, but it was just possible that something might have gone wrong—not likely, but faintly imaginable to a mind whose only chance of self-preservation had for years lain in obedience to the smallest impulses of suspicion.

There were no interrogations that night. The only object was to make Alex feel safe and welcome. But I could see in the faces of these powerful men, the true guardians of our national security, a burning interest in this bright-eyed immaculate red-headed harbinger from the country which above all might threaten that security.

A few nights later, in the same room, Alex received the biggest shock of his life. For, when he stepped inside, the first person he saw was a man he knew very well, a Russian officer who had served with him, who had been his friend. What shocked Alex, what made him freeze in unbelief, was that the man was dead! Alex himself had attended the funeral in Moscow with full military honours, and now here was his friend standing before him, alive and smiling. The funeral had been a fake by the Russians. They knew the defector had gone to the West, but dared not admit it.

When Alex had convinced himself that this was not a ghost, an Intelligence officer asked him whether he remembered another associate from the past. Yes, Alex remembered; but he never knew what happened to that man. And Captain so-and-so? Ah yes, he was killed in an aircraft crash. And General such-and-such? Oh, he died in a car accident. But now Alex was getting taut and on his guard. He imagined, quite wrongly, that this was the beginning of some formal interrogation.

It was not. For less than a week later, when he came once more to the room, he found twenty men, all Russians, whom he had known long ago. They were not dead. They were well fed and well clothed. Many had been flown from America to meet him. Others had come from the four corners of Britain.

Simply to convince Alex Penkovsky twenty men had been flown from all over the United States and Britain. They were one-time Soviet citizens, now enjoying the freedom of the West. The effect on Alex was electrical. He could hardly believe his eyes.

'We brought them along, Colonel Penkovsky, so that you may know you are among friends, that you are welcome.'

The delegation had also, for another reason, to be made welcome. For two days we saw the sights, and what sights they were for the Russians who had never before left the Soviet Union. The restaurants and shops were a fairyland, and although the allowances were meagre and the six smiling Soviets hunted chiefly in the Oxford Street Woolworth's, they window-shopped extravagantly in Bond Street and above all in Harrods. Here Alex, who alone had plenty of money, having been lavishly commissioned by generals and their wives in Moscow, bought cameras, electric razors, perfume, toilet water, talc and silk stockings by the dozen. Here, with his arms full of parcels, he first gave the cry which I was to hear so often: 'Oh, my people! My poor people!' To hear that cry was to see the bare counters and paltry windows of the Moscow stores.

But now it was time for serious business. Visits had been arranged to factories in Wolverhampton, West Hartlepool, County Durham, Birmingham, Sheffield, Leeds, Manchester, Slough and London. All arrangements had been checked by Intelligence, and in some of the factories special equipment of a tempting but valueless nature had been deliberately left in full view for the camera which it was known had been given by Pavlov at the Russian Embassy to a member of the delegation. It amused me to see this man making excuses to dodge back to see some bench, his camera concealed in his hand, when I knew that the equipment which caught his eye had been put there specially for him.

Alex entered the game with gusto. When asked by Pavlov whether he considered that the bourgeois Wynne could be bribed to obtain 'through his friends and contacts' a piece of computer equipment that was on the Soviet 'wanted' list, Alex said he was confident that this could be arranged. When he told me I requested and was given an out-of-date model of the type required, and this I took myself to the yard outside the Soviet Embassy, where I handed it over to Alex. The bribe was £50, which Alex gave to me and I gave to British Intelligence. They told me to keep it for my pains.

The visits all went smoothly, the Russians snooping away like sparrows, and Alex impatient to get back to the operations room where he could freely unload his brimming memory.

My only disgust was at the subservience of petty factory officials and junior managers towards their Soviet visitors. 'Your marvellous sputniks! Your superb ballet! Your great athletes! Your delicious caviare!' But never a word about your suppression of freedom, your tens of thousands of political prisoners, your secret police—or even your man who takes photographs of our equipment!

I do not suggest that we should insult our Soviet visitors, but I think we might well show, after our praises of Russian dancers, a little pride in our own freedom, our inheritance, and the inventions which have made our country the most beneficial to society that the world has ever seen.

So keen were the Intelligence officers to make use of every minute, to answer any queries from Washington or Whitehall without the slightest delay, that a system of signals was arranged to waylay us *en route*, should we happen to be on the open road when a query came through.

Thus, driving one morning with Alex and two comrades towards Leeds, I saw beside a well-known pub a car with the bonnet raised and the offside door open. This was my signal to stop at the next pub and treat the delegation to some

English beer. In the toilet I would find a message in an envelope stuck to the back of the cistern.

The message instructed me to take my visitors for lunch to a certain hotel, where Alex was to suffer a stomach upset from too much beer. We had chosen this symptom because on his second day in London he had suffered it genuinely, so that his comrades, who had teased him about it, would now accept a repeat performance without suspicion. I would then call a 'doctor', one of our own Intelligence men, and the delegation would be delayed while Alex answered the doctor's urgent queries.

To start with all went well. After two pints in the hotel bar Alex was duly overcome with the gripe. His agony was so realistic that the hotel manager, drawing me aside, said he shouldn't wonder if it were a burst appendix, such as had recently killed his brother. He summoned the porter, an enormous man, and together they hoisted Alex upstairs by the armpits and laid him on a bed, while I telephoned for the doctor, who quickly arrived, brown attaché case and all.

So far so good. But we had reckoned without the initiative of the manager. Having brooded round the foyer for an hour, fearful perhaps that the long delay in the bedroom signified an imminent death which would certainly cast a most undesirable gloom over his hotel, he made a telephone call himself, and in no time an ambulance bell was clanging outside and two serious attendants, hurrying for Alex's life, went dashing upstairs with a stretcher. The manager and I ran after them, and by sheer force of command I stopped the party outside the bedroom door. Slipping inside myself, I warned the doctor that he might have some awkward questions to face, but he had been well briefed, and opening the door with a truly Aesculapian majesty he informed the disappointed stretcher-bearers that the patient was fully recovered and congratulated the manager on this thoughtfulness.

The manager, reluctant to be dismissed from the episode which so clearly fascinated him, said with a puzzled frown: 'I don't remember you, sir. I thought I knew most of the doctors in this area.'

'I am on a course at the hospital. Just happened to catch the call.'

'They've got that wonderful doctor Macready up there. He's a specialist, of course. You may know him. He did my sinuses two years ago.'

'I know him well.'

'Don't say you are a specialist too, Doctor?'

'You might put it that way.'

'And might I ask what you specialise in?'

'Stomachs,' said the Intelligence officer.

On our return to London the days were full of official business, visits to factories and showrooms and exhibitions, and the nights, after bedtime, with the interrogations and training in the operations room. While the comrades slept, Alex would be spirited to the apartment block to explain and amplify through the long small hours not only the documents he had sent ahead by me, but also many others he had now brought himself. His memory was vast, accurate and highly disciplined, and he had a thousand secrets to tell about military dispositions and the organisation of the Soviet security services, military and civilian.

He was already trained in Intelligence, but there was still much for him to learn. Radio techniques, so that he could operate the long-range equipment that would enable him to keep contact with London. Coding procedures and the use of our latest micro-cameras. I was not often present at these sessions, but our experts told me that they had never had an apter pupil. Driven on by an obsession for the freedom of his beloved country, his energy was daemonic, and it was usually the doctor who had to order him to bed.

This love of freedom was the core of his personality. On the rare occasions when we could be alone together, an hour or two in the afternoon or the odd evening out, he could not get over his wonder at the way our people lived their lives as they pleased. In the Brompton Oratory he stood for an hour watching those who came with their private prayers. 'Religion may not give all the answers, Greville. I'm sure it doesn't. But at least it is free, it is not ordered by the State, and it gives a principle, something to guide our lives. At home we have nothing, only what the State commands.'

I took him to my house, where he met my wife and son and several of our friends. This was another astonishment for Alex, for in the Soviet Union it is forbidden to invite a foreigner to your house, and by revelling in these innocent gatherings (I introduced him simply as a visitor from Belgrade) he made them a huge success. A few bottles of wine, a game of Newmarket, a turn or two on the tiny dance floor in my lounge, and the evening was alight. He treated every girl he met as if she were the sexiest symbol he had ever seen, holding her hand and paying her the whackiest compliments, but with such charm and openness that the husbands and the boy friends never objected. Yet his gaiety could be turned off in a moment when there was work to do, and even the tiredness that follows gaiety. At 2 a.m. one morning, when eight of us came out of the Astor after a crazy party, I put him into a taxi and said, 'Sleep tight, Alex,' but he answered with a smile, 'Not yet, my boy,' and off he went for three hours in the interrogation room while I went thankfully home to bed.

A few days later the Soviet delegation went home, and Alex had to buy a large extra suitcase to hold all the highly contraband loot for the waiting generals.

'What about the Moscow Customs?' I asked.

'Don't worry, I shall go through like a dose of salts. General Serov will see to that. His wife is mad about perfume.'

I hoped this was true, for also concealed in the luggage were a powerful radio set, a coding machine, and the latest Minox camera with thousands of feet of high-sensitivity film.

Three weeks later I was again in Moscow, ostensibly to answer questions arising from the London visit and to discuss the possibility of any future exchange. At the Hotel Metropole I gave Alex thirty rolls of new film, and he gave me twenty rolls which he had taken since his return. He said it was some of the most valuable material he had yet laid hands on, including the names and activities of hundreds of Soviet agents, dossiers buried in the vaults of the G.R.U.

'How come they let you into the vaults, just like that?'

'I have access to all sorts of stuff,' he smiled. 'I have to give a lecture twice a year. Very important.'

'Suppose someone else happens to come in?'

'Not likely. I'm taken down by two armed guards. They lock me in!'

It was all very well to pass it off so lightly, but I knew what an iron nerve was needed. If he had been searched the Minox camera would have been his death warrant.

The report of the London delegation had, it seemed, met with full approval. The questions I had to answer were purely formal, showing, I guessed, that the Russians considered that once they were allowed into British factories, they could find out all they wanted without asking me. Guishiani and Levin complimented me on my arrangements for the delegates and wished me a pleasant stay in Moscow. My visa was only for ten days and I was told to enjoy myself. 'You like the opera, Mr. Veen, or the ballet? You have been working very hard, and we appreciate what you have done to establish trade between our two countries. So now have a good time. Colonel Penkovsky will see to everything.'

So Alex and I lived it up as best we could. We had some fine evenings together, though not so fine as in London. The

restaurants were a sorry sight compared to Soho, there were
no private parties, and certainly nothing like the Astor Club.

Even with his rank and credentials Alex considered it im-
prudent to invite me to his house, but I met his wife several
times for meals or at the ballet. She was a dark handsome
woman with a thoughtful sadness in her face. Alex was forbidden to tell her that he was a senior officer in the G.R.U.,
and for her own sake, in case he were caught, he breathed no
word about his work for the West. Through the long lonely
years of planning and accumulation he had kept his secret,
and how well I understood this loneliness! Now it was even
more important that she should remain ignorant. She knew
him only as a colonel in the Red Army, and he told me that
this falseness had clouded his married life. The strain of being only one person to her, when he was two others to himself, made it almost impossible for him to relax in his own
home, and relaxation was essential, if he were not to go mad
under the burden of his dangers.

'The trouble is, Greville,' he said with his charming smile,
'that I need girls, I really do. Not to give my heart to, that
would be too dangerous, but just to have a good time with.
What I need is a permanent supply of little sugar-plums to
help me forget myself.'

'There must be a few around Moscow, surely?'

'Ah, but you have to be so careful, so very careful. For instance, there's a girl called Tania, but I daren't meet her
more than once a month, and then it has to be in holes and
corners. The G.R.U. don't like this sort of thing, and, apart
from that, she might be a plant. It's always possible.'

'Who is she, a dancer?'

'No, she works in what you would call the Foreign Office.
And, oh boy, you should see her figure!'

'Why not get her along tonight? It might be fun.'

'Good God, no. You and I are probably watched wherever
we go, and we certainly mustn't be seen with Tania. Besides,

she's a clever little thing. If she saw how well you and I get on together she might start thinking—and that would never do.'

If the girl situation was difficult for Alex it was still more difficult for foreign visitors. At the American House Club I met a visiting scientist from Scandinavia. Let us call him Rex. He was, it appeared, a gay cavalier, and accustomed to plenty of amour wherever he went. He was a living contradiction of the rumour that scientists are inhuman. This was his first visit to Moscow, and he did not see why his usual practice should be suspended, so in spite of all warnings and discouragements he quickly found himself a beautiful girl, a member of the ballet school, whose most striking feature was the long blue-black hair which she wore piled up into a captivating top-knot. They met almost every night, and after a late dinner Rex would take her back to his hotel and up to his room. He knew this was forbidden, but in his infatuation believed that his fame as a scientist gave him immunity from the prying eyes of the porter.

Inevitably (in the strictest confidence, of course, that most certain of all methods of dissemination) Rex boasted to me of the ballet girl's charms. I even saw the happy couple as I dined alone one evening when Alex was absent on some official business. I could understand Rex's enthusiasm. She was one of the few really disturbing girls I had seen in Moscow.

When I told Alex he hit the table with his hand:

'Ballet school? Hair on top? It sounds like . . . no, it can't be. That would be too fantastic! Still, we can soon find out. Come on, Greville, this is going to be fun.'

He took me to a dark street where we hid in a doorway to watch the house opposite.

'We're lucky it's Thursday,' said Alex.

'Why?'

'Because I happen to know that a certain dancer had a

date in that house tonight at nine o'clock. It's 9.30 now. We shouldn't have long to wait.'

'Who is the man?'

'You'll see. She'll come out first, and he will follow about five minutes later.'

It was as Alex had predicted. At ten minutes to ten a girl came out of the door opposite and walked quickly down the street. It was dark, but in the dim glow from a window I had no doubt that she was Rex's companion. Five minutes later the door opened again and a sturdy figure muffled in greatcoat and fur hat moved slowly away with the heavy serious steps of a man who has had enough.

'Who was that?' I asked.

'It was Levin!'

'The naughty boy! I wonder what General Serov would say!'

I do not usually interfere in romance, but I felt it my duty, for security reasons, to report to London that one of the scientists from a friendly nation was regularly going to bed with the girl friend of one of the trusted assistants to the Head of Soviet Military Intelligence.

The reaction was almost instantaneous, and Rex found himself in an aircraft heading for home.

For the man who needs oats Moscow is a place to avoid. For foreigners an easy pick-up is almost certain to be an agent of Civilian Security, the K.G.B., while for Russian citizens the normal routines of courtship are strictly discouraged. There is nowhere for young people to go. Kissing or holding hands in public is forbidden, petting in cinemas would probably mean arrest, and young couples could not take a hotel room without surrendering their identification papers. In Gorky Park a young couple can hardly sit down before they are moved on by the police. Brothels are unknown and there is no call-girl system. There are not enough telephones anyway.

One Soviet concession is the line of taxis outside the Hotel Moscow. In the back of each taxi sits a girl, and if you fancy a ride out to the woods near the airport you must approach the leading taxi. If you cannot speak Russian the driver will slam in the gear and drive round the block to take station astern at the other end of the line. If you are Russian, or your Russian is fluent and you are prepared to take the risk, you may climb in the back and be driven to the dark woods, where, for a handsome quantity of roubles, the driver will go for a walk.

I watched this pantomime one night with Alex. We saw the approaches, the rejections, and the occasional dive into the taxi for the sordid and uncomfortable journey of love. The average was four rejections to one acceptance, from which one may perhaps deduce that foreigners, if not four times as potent, are at least four times more desperate than the regimented citizens of Moscow.

The only real encouragement towards sex comes from the Security Services, especially the K.G.B., who use it as a possible means of blackmail. Any foreign visitor who is of technical or political importance in his own country will be studied carefully for his weaknesses. If he is homosexual or a womaniser he will be provided with all he desires until, by photographs and tape-recordings, he is fully compromised. A taste for alcohol, or better still drugs, can also lead to the point of no return.

Although at this time I was, so far as I could judge, entirely accepted by the Scientific Research Committee, I was one evening offered the treatment which I assumed was no result of suspicion but simply the normal K.G.B. routine.

Having said good night to Alex I went up to my room and found in my bed a dark smiling girl with hefty shoulders and an odour that came from no bottle. Her dress was over a chair. I had been half expecting such a visitor and had already rehearsed with myself what to do. Without saying a word, without closing the door, I shot downstairs and told the desk clerk, as he slumped behind his *Pravda*, that the accommodation desk had made an unfortunate mistake. My room had been let, clearly by some error of duplication, to an unknown lady. I would take a short walk while this error was put right.

I was never visited again and no mention was made of the incident. When I told Alex he said, 'They were only trying it on. You did the right thing, of course, but it's rather a shame that Soviet hospitality cannot be trusted!'

Before I left Moscow we had two pieces of good news. First, that in July Alex would be coming again to London for the Soviet Trade Exhibition at Earls Court, and would accompany Madame Serov on a short social visit. And, second, that in September there was to be a Soviet Trade Fair in Paris with the possibility of Alex being present and an unsolicited invitation for me. The next time Levin saw me in Gorky Street he said: 'We hope that you will come to our fair, Mr. Veen. It is going to be the greatest exhibition ever seen in Europe. We shall be delighted to welcome you!' And I would be delighted to attend, for although it was good when I could get to Moscow and bring back Alex's films and papers, it was better when Alex could come West where the full team of Allied Intelligence would be waiting.

This looked like being a great year and everything seemed possible. Walking in Gorky Park on our last afternoon, the flowering trees were in full blossom and the sun was warm. Standing under an immense chestnut tree whose pink clusters hung heavy and still against the clear sky, Alex breathed in deeply and flung his arms wide as if he would embrace the air.

'Greville, there's nothing we can't achieve, nothing at all.'
'Don't talk like that,' I said, 'it's not good.'
'Nonsense, it's wonderful. Think of London—and Paris —just think of it.'

I thought of it during the month of June when I was back in London waiting for Alex to arrive. My training went on at full pressure. I had courses to attend in coding, tape-recording and communications, and a continental insistence on the basic principles which I had first learnt during the war. Such as:

Observing physical characteristics of people I met.

Remembering names and occupations.

When meeting a colleague in public always to shield the lips with a hand or a glass, to prevent lip-reading by a stranger. An expert lip-reader can follow ninety per cent of a conversation from the far side of a room.

When passing messages never to do so at arm's length but always close to the other person.

For a rendezvous always to inspect the area beforehand, and never to arrive early or late. If the contact is missing, never to hang about, but to go away and return at pre-arranged intervals. To have an alternative place of rendezvous.

To choose the sites for dead-letter boxes in places where the picker-up could be seen without suspicion, such as grave-yards, public gardens, or the entrance halls of buildings, and to vary the sites frequently.

When on an assignment, never to mix with the friends of everyday life, and, if such a meeting unexpectedly occurs, to break it up as quickly as possible.

To study and memorise photograph albums and descriptions of known Russian agents, and always to be on the look-out for them, especially at places of rendezvous.

Such were some of the principles, and I absorbed them in theory and practice till they became second nature. Trial runs of every kind were arranged for me, and I could feel my memory improving and my alertness getting sharper.

When Alex came in July his duties at the Trade Exhibition were not arduous. His only other job was to escort

Madame Serov, but this was a task which the Soviet Embassy staff were only too anxious to share. Pavlov and his friends vied with each other to entertain the wife of the great general, and this meant that Alex, though his stay was shorter than in April had more spare time.

He was staying at a hotel in Kensington where an operations room was set up in a nearby apartment block, as on his last visit. Back among friends, his confidence and energy appeared limitless, and the Intelligence boys told me that they had nicknamed him 'the sleepless wonder'. It was towards the end of this visit that I had an unusual experience.

The Intelligence chiefs had by now had time to analyse the material which Alex had given them. It was an impressive mass, and whatever doubts they may have had, before they met Alex, about his integrity and value, they had no doubts now. He had already given military and technical data of the highest importance and there was more to come.

I knew the outline but not all the details. My job was to keep the pipeline open, but the vital facts and figures were for other ears than mine. There was one type of information, however, which directly concerned me, for Alex, trained by the G.R.U., knew all the latest Soviet methods of interrogating political prisoners, and although the general principles were already familiar to my people, it was decided that Alex's up-to-date knowledge might be used to my advantage.

'It's just an idea, Greville,' said my chief one morning, 'and you are perfectly free to decline if you wish. But we have been thinking that supposing things ever went wrong for you, it might help you to have sampled what is likely to happen. We could provide a sort of endurance test, but . . .'

'That sounds fine,' I said.

'Now wait a minute. Don't rush it. Go away and think it over. You would be in the hands of people you've never seen and who don't know who you are. It wouldn't be exactly pleasant, I daresay.'

'I can see the point though.'

'Good. Well, sleep on it anyway.'

Next morning I went back and announced cheerfully: 'Well, I'm ready for the rehearsal.'

'Don't let's be macabre,' said the chief. 'A rehearsal implies a performance, and the odds are this will never happen. But just in case . . . I think you are wise to take this opportunity.'

'How long will I be there?'

'You'll find out,' said the chief.

A few days later I was taken by car to a house in the country, isolated in the hills. We arrived at about three in the afternoon.

I had a quick impression of desolation. Weeds and flaking stucco. Attached to the house was a garage with a room built on top.

The moment I came into the entrance hall I was grabbed by a six-foot, fifteen stone, red-faced, bulging-necked character who rushed me upstairs, along a corridor and into the room over the garage. The room had a stone floor, cement walls, and no furniture. The only light was through a tiny window too high to reach, with a metal shutter, at the moment open, which I saw was controlled from the corridor by a wire running along the ceiling.

No word was spoken. I was left alone, the door was locked, and after a few minutes the shutter slid over the window and I was in darkness. I had my cigarettes, lighter and watch, so I sat on the floor and smoked and got hungry. At eleven o'clock Red-face came in with two other men. My watch was taken, my clothes ripped off, and I was alone again, but this time naked. It was not freezing but it was very cold, and a musty dampness oozed into my bones. I wanted to urinate, but when I banged on the door there was no answer, so I chose a corner and then lay down as far away as I could get. I slept in the end, but I kept waking up, reaching for bedclothes with my back raw from the grit. It was worse on my side because the hip bone seemed to pierce the skin. I had never been so long without food and water. There was sand-paper in my throat and a hot pincer in my stomach.

Time was hard to calculate in the darkness, but I fancied it was about noon next day when the door opened and Red-face came in with his two henchmen and I was dragged along to another room and dumped on a chair with a bright light in my face.

'All right,' said Red-face, 'now let's hear all about it.'

'All about what?'

For an answer I was picked up from behind and hurled on the floor. As I went down, the side of a hard hand hit the muscle in my neck. I was lifted on to the chair, and Red-face said:

'We know that you were approached by the Soviet Em-bassy and we know you agreed to work for them. We have proof of that. All we require at the moment is a few details, and there's no sense in stalling, because you won't leave here till we get them.'

'You're mistaken,' I said, and down I went again, but this time with a punch between the shoulder blades and a slap in the liver. These men were experts, they knew how to hurt without leaving marks.

For about an hour this treatment continued. The line of questions showed that they considered me to be a double agent working for the Soviets. And I had the nasty feeling that they really believed this. Red-face was clearly too thick to be an actor. He had been told to use these methods to break down my resistance as quickly as possible, and he in-tended to do it. When I denied what he was suggesting I was man-handled, and when they took me back to the stone room I collapsed on the floor.

Two hours later I was fetched again for interrogation, and this went on at regular short intervals, till I lost all sense of time and wished to God that I had declined the experiment. I could not be sure, but it felt about three days before I was given my first food, a bowl of weak gruel and some tea without milk or sugar. The shutter was opened and a thin light fell across the high ceiling. The room stank with my urinations, and now, weak and confused, with a splitting headache, a horrible thought came to my mind.

Suppose this were not an experiment in training but a genuine investigation? Suppose British Intelligence, who I had always supposed trusted me, did not trust me? Suppose they believed that when I had told them about my dealings with Pavlov and Kulikov I was only telling half the truth? I know that this was not logical, but I was learning that when the body is beaten and starved the mind loses its logic.

For a long time I sat against the wall. I was naked, forsaken, and frightened. Before I could sort out my thoughts and all that they implied I was hauled off for another interrogation, but as I was thrust down on to the chair with the light in my face I stopped feeling sorry for myself and was overcome with a sudden fury. At the first clout on my neck I told Red-face what I thought of him, and when he said that I would not leave the house till I signed a statement that I had not been manhandled in any way I replied in my most fruity army language. The result was another beating, and as I was dragged to the door, I looked back and saw on the red face an expression of animal satisfaction. It was possible that he had been told to behave like this. It was equally possible that he had only been told to do the job which he so clearly relished. Whichever it was, I was the loser.

But by now I was almost an animal myself. I stopped thinking because there was nothing profitable to think about.

The interrogation became simple sequences of statement, denial, and assault. No variation and no progress. Once a day I was given gruel and tea. I was unshaven. My body was dirty, stinking, cold and bruised. I was not frightened of

Red-face any more, I was not even obstinate, I was relaxed. I had the apathy of a carcass. For about another three days I shuffled from the bright light to the darkness, to and fro. My only positive thoughts were directed with savage reproach towards my chief and his colleagues. You rotten bastards! You mistrusting sons of bitches! You sadists! Where did you find him? In an ape-house? Or a glass-house? That's it, he was an army prison warder and got chucked out for being so twisted. You're all twisted, you're a lousy shower of twisted, disloyal, sadistical, unintelligent, illegitimate sons of . . .

'Hello, Greville! How's tricks?'

In the open doorway stood two of my Intelligence friends. They had natty suits and smiles.

'I can't ask you to sit down,' I said, 'unless you like the floor.'

'Not to worry. We thought you might be ready for a spot of dinner.'

They stood aside, and Red-face conducted me without a word to a shower room where new clothes had been laid out.

My friends were waiting in a new Bentley. We drove a few miles to a cosy log-fired inn where a magnificent dinner was served. Something warned me not to overload my unpractised stomach, but I neglected the warning. I shovelled down all the food and drink I could hold. It was a great evening. There was no mention, either then or afterwards, of my visit to the house in the hills. The test was over, and now there were more important things to be thought of.

That night I was as sick as a dog.

Alex had only a few days left. I had not seen much of him during this visit, but three episodes are worth recall.

The first, when our people suggested that, to impress the Soviet Embassy, he might inspect the tomb of Karl Marx in Highgate. We found the tombstone mildewed and the grave overgrown with weeds. Alex, as a good member of the Communist Party, made a report to Moscow, who in turn sent a severe letter to Pavlov at the Soviet Embassy, and a note of congratulations to Comrade Penkovsky.

The second, at breakfast one Sunday morning in the Kensington hotel where I had joined him.

Alex adored the pretty girls of London, but there was another type who fascinated him equally. These were the middle-aged, well-bred, slightly stuffy spinsters, the daughters of important men, now living on shrinking incomes but with the arrogance and attitudes of a bygone age.

Two such ladies, dressed with expensive unsmartness, sat at the next table. They were swapping their anecdotes with such piercing elocution that we could do nothing but listen to every word. For some time they babbled of libraries and dogs, and then, when the inevitable question of going to church arose, one of them was reminded of what she called 'my funny story' (as if they had not all been that), and after a long irrelevancy about the table silver at a house where she had stayed once for the weekend, she went on, with her voice rising to shrieks at the key words . . . 'So when it came to Sunday morning Laura said was I coming to church, and of course I said yes, I mean I *was* her guest, wasn't I, and when we got there I found to my *horror* that the service was very very high indeed, so after about half an hour of chanting—and, my dear, my nose was absolutely *dazed* with the smell—someone rang a bell and everyone dropped on their knees, well at that I *simply* revolted, I thought I'm blowed if I'm going to do *this* sort of thing, after all I am a good honest *Christian*, aren't I, so I just *stood* quite firmly, I felt rather awful, but then I noticed another lady who was standing up near the front, and I thought well thank goodness for at least *someone* else with some sense, so when the service was over I waited for her by the door. She was a tall lady quite well dressed, and I said to her, "Excuse me, but I am *so* delighted to find another good honest Christian who refuses to kneel down all the time", and my dear, she simply hissed one word at me ... ARTHRITIS ! '

For a long time afterwards, whenever we felt dull or there was a pause in the conversation, Alex would hiss in his beautiful Russian voice 'ARTHRITIS!' and collapse with laughter.

The third episode was when Alex said he would like to see British justice at work, and in the absence of any spectacular murder trial I took him to a complicated financial case where a director was accused of swindling his company out of £30,000. The defence barrister made what seemed a very dull and unconvincing plea based on a number of technical quibbles. I thought the defendant clearly guilty, and so did the prosecutor, who delivered a resounding final tirade with great gusto and sat down with evident satisfaction. But the judge, summing up in his quiet dry voice, reminded the jury that appearances were not enough for conviction and that they might well think that the arguments by defence offered enough room for a positive doubt. The jury, after half an hour away, brought in a verdict of 'not guilty'.

When we came out Alex who had listened spellbound to every word was almost in tears. 'That could never have happened in Russia,' he said. 'He was obviously guilty. He was acquitted on technicalities.'

'I thought so too.'

'But he was declared innocent because he was not proved guilty. That is the thing to remember. That is the most wonderful thing I have ever seen in my life.'

# 3
# Trial

## I

IT IS one of the General's bad mornings. He does not offer me a cigarette. When he has finished speaking the interpreter says:

'You have been in Lubyanka for five months. You still show no signs of co-operating. It is very foolish of you. If you persist in this attitude you may well find that when your trial comes it will take place *in camera*. We are not obliged to allow criminals of your sort to tell their lies in public.'

'My trial? And when is that going to be?'

'It will be when we are ready, which depends largely on you. So now—let us try to be more reasonable. We know, for instance, that you organised agents in the Soviet Union. Who were they? What were their names?'

'I did not organise agents. That is not part of a business-man's job.'

'You are lying. We know who the agents were, we only ask you to tell us your part in their organisation.'

'I am afraid that I cannot tell what never took place.'

This is the old routine. We have been through this sort of conversation many times before. But here the General has made a mistake, for it is not true that I organised agents, and by stating that he knows I did it, the General is showing me that he is not sure what my exact function and duties really were. I am pleased that the General is confused, but it is only a slight pleasure, because I am very weak and tired these days. My food is bad and my exercise irregular. For over a fortnight now, since I saw Alex being dragged away by the two massive guards, the interrogations have been long and continuous. At all hours of the day and night I have been brought up and forced to stand with a bright light in my face, and the room full of civilians who I guess to be from the K.G.B., hostile characters chipping in with questions which the General repeats and the interpreter passes on. The whole proceedings are being taken down on tape. I am pretty sure of this because about every half-hour there is a break, and the Lieutenant-Colonel leaves the room for a few minutes, and I do not know what he can be doing except changing the tapes. The microphones are concealed, but I am sure they are somewhere. Later on some poor bastard will have to type out the endless hours of question and denial, and the General will have to sweat through the typescript and make a report, and the report will be studied by dozens of Intelligence officers. I cannot see what they will get out of it except frustration.

But now one of the K.G.B. men says something, and a tape-recorder is brought in, and I am ordered to listen to one of my actual conversations with 'the traitor Penkovsky'. They are our voices all right, and I remember where we were talking, in a room in the Ukraine Hotel. We had turned on the television and also a radio loudspeaker, but now the voices come through quite clearly with the music in the background. It is technically interesting that they have been able to separate the voices from the loud music, but I am not pleased to have made such an error. At the time we thought we were safe, but we were wrong, and now all I can do is to stand and listen to myself asking Alex whether everything is all right, and Alex saying he has received details about plans for his escape from the Union, should it become necessary, and me asking if there were any interesting methods, and Alex saying that one idea was to get him out by submarine.

I know, of course, that it is possible to cut tapes and fake conversations which never took place, but in this case it has not been necessary because what we had said was bad enough without adjustments.

'So what is your answer to that?' enquires the General. 'I suppose you are going to deny that it was your voice you've been listening to?'

I have no answer. The General has made his point. Now he is in a better mood and goes on:

'Well, that is something. At least you have not denied the truth for once. Now here are some photographs. Look at them and tell us who all these people are who can be seen talking to you in the streets of Moscow.'

The photographs show me talking to various Russians whose names I never knew. I do not even recognise their faces, though I remember the sort of occasion. Sometimes it would be a citizen who simply wanted a chat with a Westerner, sometimes a student who was asking for souvenirs, or anxious to do a black market deal of some kind. I tell the General that I do not know their names but that they were Soviet citizens who wished to talk to me and stopped me in the street.

'Why should our honest Soviet people wish to talk to you?' roars the General. 'The truth is that you were trying to spread your filthy Western propaganda among our students. Well, let me tell you, Mr. Veen, that a foreigner like you may come here once without being checked. Maybe twice. But *never* three times.'

He is hinting at the dossiers which are made on every regular foreigner. Alex himself contributed to my dossier. He showed me his contributions. Members of the Soviet delegation to London wrote their impressions of me. Alex showed me these too.

There was another precaution by the Soviets. In my early visits to Moscow, before I went to the Scientific Research Committee and met their permanent chiefs, my experience has been that you rarely, among the minor officials, meet the same man twice. You meet a man and try to establish a good relationship with him, and think you are getting along fine but, the next time you visit his office, the chances are that you will be interviewed by someone else. It seems a general Soviet principle to discourage any firm and lasting contact between their own officials and businessmen from other countries.

I do not answer the General back because I am tired and my leg is hurting. I have found that silence is often the best way of bringing the interrogation to an end. But this morning the General has his talking boots on.

'When will you understand,' he shouts, 'that we will never allow a foreigner to come and start his dirty work of espionage in the Soviet Union? Such things are repulsive to us, utterly repulsive.'

'They are not repulsive to your colleagues in London,' I say.

'What's that? What are you talking about now?'

'I'm simply telling you, with the greatest respect, that a member of your Embassy in London approached me to ask whether I would obtain scientific information for the Soviet Union.'

'Lies!' screams the General. 'How could you possibly ob-tain such information? You are only a salesman, that is all.'

'I am glad to hear you say so,' I reply. 'I had rather got the idea that you imagined I was a spy.'

'You are a salesman who is prepared to act as a spy. And who was this man at our Embassy whom you falsely accuse of making such a ridiculous request?'

'His name was Kulikov. He worked under Pavlov.'

Now the General gets sarcastic: 'We do not make use of

our foreign embassies, like you do yours, as centres of espionage. But if it were true—which it is not—that such an approach had been made to you, it is very surprising that you did not jump at the chance of making a little money for yourself, just as you certainly jumped at the chance to come to the Soviet Union and, for the sake of some paltry reward, to abuse our friendship and hospitality, as is shown by your guilty silence when we show you photographs and tape recordings of your dealings with the traitor Penkovsky.'

The General is very pleased with this oratory, but I do not answer back, and after another hour of my occasional short denials and my frequent shrugs and silences, even the K.G.B. men are shuffling and looking at their watches, and the General says, 'All right, Mr. Veen, that is enough. But don't forget—if you expect us to go to the expense of a trial in open court, with the Press of the world attending you will have to co-operate,' and I am taken back to my cell.

It is necessary to me that the trial be in open court, for after a trial *in camera* our people would never know how much the Soviets had found out. There may not be much opportunity. I cannot see the Russians allowing me to say what I like, but the question is, how far can they stop me? There may be ways for me to slip in some remarks which the journalists will understand. I shall have to wait and see. In the meantime my plan is to relax a little, to play along with the General at least enough to ensure an open trial. That is my plan, but now two snags appear.

The first is when, a few mornings later, Alex is brought into the interrogation room, and we are left alone with two guards. There are the hidden microphones, of course, but we do not worry about these because we are not going to talk secrets.

It is not Alex any more, but a hollow echo of Alex. The light has gone from his eyes. They are dull and bloodshot. The music has gone from his voice, and the strength from his hands and face. We sit at a small table. He glances at me, then looks away and says slowly:

'Greville, they are talking about having the trial *in camera*. That would be fatal. The trial must be in open court.'

'I think it will be. They do not wish to be accused of rigging the evidence. Besides, they would hardly stoop to such a thing, there is no need.'

I put it this way because of the microphones.

'But they are afraid,' says Alex, 'that you will make trouble in the open court. If you do that, the trial will be taken *in camera*, and if that happens, I will be shot.'

'Now, Alex . . .'

'No, no, it is true. They have promised me my life, providing that I tell the truth in open court. They know everything about me. I was caught with all the evidence, and I have told them everything that happened, everything!'

When Alex says this, he looks at me, and strokes the back of his neck. The sign again! He is telling me that he has confessed about his own activities but not about mine. He has kept faithfully to the story that I was a businessman and nothing else. I know already that he has kept faith, from the sign he made weeks ago with his rubbing fingers, but now he is confirming this.

'You have told the truth,' I say, 'and so have I. What more can they expect?'

'But don't you understand? They have got to be convinced that you are not going to make trouble in the court, that you are not going to make a whole lot of anti-Soviet statements. And now I am asking you the same thing, for my own sake.'

His voice is weak and desperate. When I think of the old Alex, the Alex who strode through Customs with the heavy suitcases, who steamed round Moscow like a marathon walker, who flung up his strong arms under the chestnut tree in Gorky Park, who laughed, who drank, who adored pretty girls. When I think of all this, I feel the whole world is poisoned that such things can happen. But the poison is Soviet, I have to remember that. These people cannot, shall not, corrupt me through sentiment, powerful though it is. I say quietly:

'Now look, Alex—I sympathise with you. I am sorry it has come to this, very sorry indeed. But you cannot expect me to stand up in open court and confess to crimes which I never committed, or say how wonderful everything is in the Soviet Union, which I do not believe. I must tell the truth, I have my own country and my own way of life to protect. I am not a hero, but I will never betray my country, because I have seen how Communism works, and I don't like it.'

'I'm only asking you not to make trouble, that is all. My life depends on that. I'm asking you for my life.'

I nod, because I cannot think of what to say. I would like to tell Alex that I intend at the trial to make contact with the outside world, but not in a way that will damage him. But I cannot say this into the microphones, so I smile at him and nod my head.

'Promise me, Greville. I want to hear you say it.'

'I promise.'

Now Alex is taken away and I do not see him again till we meet in the courtroom.

The trial cannot be very far away, I think, because suddenly my food improves. I have complained often enough about feeling sick and weak, but now a doctor appears who announces that I need more nourishment. It does not need a genius to see this, but the order, as always in the Soviet Union, must be given by the correct authority. So now I can be fattened up a little for the trial. I have meat or fish every day, I have milk, I have white bread, I have eggs for breakfast, and even a sausage or two. Heavens, Bond, another month of this and I shall be fit to tear open a couple of steel doors and escape from Lubyanka!

Some days after my food improves I have positive confirmation that the trial is approaching, when one morning I see some new faces in the interrogation room, and I am told that is the team for the prosecution. The chief prosecutor is even coarser, larger and louder than the General himself. The prosecutor takes over questioning and at once starts shouting at me, but I am an old hand by now at being shouted at, and whenever the prosecutor finishes speaking, I talk very quietly to the interpreter and pretend that I do not understand what he says, and may I have a repeat, and would he be kind enough to ask the prosecutor to begin all over again, and so on, which makes the prosecutor yell and bluster all the more, and I see the General frowning to himself. On the third day there is such a row going on that finally I say, 'Please be good enough to tell the prosecutor not to shout at me. I can't understand a word he says anyway. By making all this noise he is getting nothing out of me and is only distressing himself.' When the interpreter passes this on, the prosecutor, who has been slapping his palm with a ruler, gives a cry of despair and hurls the ruler on the table and, bringing a pill bottle out of his pocket, he gulps down two pills with a glass of water.

Next day a new prosecutor appears and he too begins by shouting, but when I do my softly-softly routine he quietens down and is evidently more acceptable to the General. It is not much of a victory, in fact it is no victory at all, because I know that when the trial comes they will say and do what they have decided, and whoever is prosecutor will only be acting on orders.

Likewise with the counsel for defence. This is a man named Borovik, who is produced with a great flourish: 'Here is Mr. Borovik, who will be conducting your defence. You may have five minutes alone with him, to see how you get on together.'

When we are alone I say: 'Well, Mr. Borovik, this is all a

great waste of time. Is there truthfully anything whatever that you can do for me?'

'But I am a trained lawyer, Mr. Veen. I come from the Central Legal Bureau in Moscow, and I am here to defend you.'

Before the five minutes is up, the others come back, and the General asks me whether I am satisfied with my counsel, and I say no, I have a much better man in London, but there is no reaction to this quip and the questions go on, with Borovik standing with his chin in his hand, as if he is making grave decisions about my defence.

During these days of preparation one point arises which, though it does not concern me directly, I see is of the utmost importance. This is when the prosecuter says that Penkovsky has confessed to having been received in London by certain persons of very high standing. Now I happen to know that this is true. I knew at the time that Alex was meeting them, and I know that it will be a very bad thing if news of that meeting comes out at the trial. It would create the rumpus of all rumpuses in Britain if it were to appear that these persons, though they only met Alex socially, had given their blessing to him or to anyone connected with him. And the prosecutor knows this as well as I do.

'Well, Mr. Veen,' he says, 'this is very interesting, is it not? And we must not forget, must we, that the Press of the world will be attending the trial?'

Now here, once more, I have to think very fast, and to give myself a little time I say casually:

'Colonel Penkovsky may have said that this meeting took place, I know nothing about it. Anyhow I cannot see at the moment why it should be of any special interest to anyone. He met many people in London, no doubt.'

'Now come, Mr. Veen. These are not ordinary people, are they? Suppose it was up to you. Would you decide it was good for all this to be reported in the newspapers all over the world? You are a criminal, but you are not a fool. So what do you say?'

I have nothing to say. My mind is blank, and I am still trying to appear unconcerned, as if the whole matter were too trivial to be discussed, when to my astonishment the prosecutor solves my problem for me.

'I mention these important people,' he says, 'because we are prepared to make a bargain with you. It is entirely one-sided, of course. You will gain much and we shall gain very little. It is only another example of how, in the face of your obstinacy, we are ready to be reasonable.'

'What is it that you propose?'

'Well, it is a small domestic point concerning Penkovsky. For reasons which don't concern you we would prefer that, if we decide to grant you an open trial, you do not say in court that Penkovsky was a member of the Communist Party, nor that he was an Intelligence officer in the G.R.U. It is of no great importance, but if you agree to keep quiet about this, we will promise not to say anything about that embarrassing meeting in London.'

I do not believe in Soviet promises but here I have no choice. If there is the smallest chance of silence about the meeting I must take it. So I say casually: 'Very well, I will do as you wish. It does not matter much either way, so I will agree to what you ask.'

I know it is important to the Soviets that the image of their authority should not be damaged by the news that a Party member and an officer of the G.R.U. has betrayed them. Whether they can keep a promise is another matter.

But the smooth must be taken with the rough, and I have to record that during the actual trial no mention was made of the meeting whose publication I so desperately wished to avoid.

But now, at the last moment, the second snag appears

which is going to hinder my plan for making contact with the outside world.

This snag, which I have not foreseen, is that I am rehearsed for the trial. I am given my civilian clothes and allowed to use my electric razor and after breakfast when I am spruced up I am taken in a prison van to the building of the Soviet Supreme Court.

In the courtroom I am met by Borovik, who, while we are waiting for the prosecutor, starts telling me how hard he has been working on my case, how he has perused the notes of my interrogations and is determined to make a good defence. I do not pay much attention to Borovik because I have no faith either in him or in Soviet justice, and after a while he stops his yarn and gives me a bar of chocolate, which I eat quickly because I am getting nervous. This is my arena, this is the place of decision for which I have been heading for the last seven months of weary interrogation. It is a large room, almost empty at the moment, but when full it will hold several hundred people. Now odd characters begin to come in, who, I am told, are stand-ins for the officials of court, one for the judge, another for the clerk of court and so on. Someone is fiddling with a headset and mouthpiece in the dock. These are for me, so that I may hear a translation of all that is said. Then the prosecutor comes in, and I am put in the dock and given a bulky typescript which turns out to be a complete word-for-word rendering not only of questions that will be put to me, but of my answers.

I protest at this, but the prosecutor says shortly that the prisoner will do what he is told, and that any attempt to depart from the typed answers will be treated as contempt of court and may result in the trial being sent into *camera*.

There is clearly nothing to be done about this, and I do not protest any more because I suddenly realise that, if the reporters from the outside world see me reading answers off a typescript, they will need no help from me to conclude that the trial is a farce, and part of my object will be achieved.

But I am quickly disillusioned for, as soon as I sit down, the prosecutor says that I will be required to learn my answers by heart during the rehearsals so that when the trial comes I shall not need any notes.

'Excuse me,' I say, 'but I am not a trained actor. My memory is not good, and I have never been accustomed to learning things by heart, certainly not documents of this length.'

'The prisoner will comply with orders.'

'I am sorry. I do not wish to disobey orders,' (not much!) 'but I can tell you now that this task is completely beyond me. I cannot learn all this. There are over a hundred pages.'

There is a hurried discussion among the prosecution team, and then the prosecutor says: 'Very well, the prisoner may retain the notes, but they must be kept out of sight on the shelf in front of him.'

This is not so good but it may be better than nothing. At the trial I shall have to make a show of bending my head and looking up again, so that the reporters will know I am reading off notes, but at the moment I must keep this plan to myself. The rehearsal is about to start and I shall need all my concentration to follow the arguments, such as they may be, and to learn exactly of what it is that I am to be accused.

For the next six hours, with a short break for a meal, I am taken through my part. After the prosecutor speaks I hear the voice of the interpreter in my headset, and after I have spoken into the mouthpiece the interpreter repeats in Russian. My voice is fairly well amplified, but I keep it down because at the trial I plan to speak as loudly as possible, to make sure that the Press, who will be seated at the far end of the hall, shall hear.

It is explained to me that the questions for rehearsal will not constitute the whole trial, but only those important questions on which I shall be obliged to give the answers required.

Apart from this, I shall certainly be cross-examined and shall then be free to give my own answers, except that the freedom must remain within the bounds of my promise not to make trouble or say things against the Soviet Union. Some freedom! Still, there may be loopholes, I shall have to wait and see. I shall have to calculate how far I can go without ending up *in camera*.

The rehearsal is long and tiring, and from it I learn two main points. One, that they have extracted from Alex an extraordinarily accurate but by no means full account of the times and places we met, and the contents of the packages we exchanged and that these, together with the information supplied by photographs and microphones, constitute an undeniable picture of my actions, though not of my motives or knowledge. And two, that I am presented as a frightened businessman who, at first unwittingly and later unwillingly, was drawn into the operation as a courier for Alex, and above all that although I am a degenerate Westerner myself, I still was disgusted by the even greater degeneracy of Penkovsky. The question of whether I knew all that was going on is not yet 'proved' by the answers I am instructed to give, and will clearly depend on cross-examination. The whole purpose of the trial is to attack Penkovsky. He is the villain, and I, though I will be dealt with as a criminal against the Soviet Union, am chiefly to be used as an instrument to show to what depths he sank.

I can understand this. If a colonel in the Grenadier Guards were found guilty of giving secrets to a foreign power his activities would naturally take headline precedence in Britain over the machinations of some worthless assistant from the Balkans. I understand, but it is little comfort. I shall get no favours, worthless and subsidiary though I may be.

The next day there is another rehearsal and we go through the whole thing several times more. 'Speak clearly and naturally. Do not look at your notes so much. You should

know most of them by now. Do not attempt to say anything
that is not in the notes.' I am drilled till my brain flags and I
feel almost an automaton.

The third day is the dress rehearsal. I am taken by car
this morning and, though the windows are curtained, I see
through the windscreen that the streets near the courthouse
are barricaded and signposted as if some diversion of traffic
has been planned. The officers of the court are present themselves in the courtroom and there is an increasing tension
and atmosphere of deadly seriousness.

When I arrive Alex is there. He is being taken through his
part in Russian, which is not translated for my benefit. He
looks a little better than when I last saw him, but only as a
mild convalescent would look after a long illness. He has lost
his erectness and, though his cheeks have a little colour, his
eyes are moist and dim. We have no chance to speak and
when he has finished, he is taken out and I am in the dock
once more, but this time with the full attention of the judge
and the full blast from the prosecutor who seems to be working himself up towards a mighty display of eloquence. I feel
unreal. To be rehearsed in what by all standards of justice
should be spontaneous gives me the sensation of taking part
in a nightmare. They might as well cut all this palaver and
sentence me on the spot. But I try to quell these feelings and
to concentrate on saving my energy for the trial itself.

Late that afternoon, when the rehearsal is over, Borovik
comes to see me in an anteroom. He brings some of the trial
documents and papers, which have been translated into English. He asks me to sign that I have read them, but I refuse
to sign. I point out that many of the statements which I am
supposed to make are untrue.

'That is not the question,' says Borovik. 'You are simply
signing that the translation is accurate and that you have
read the documents.'

'I have never signed anything for my interrogators. I do not intend to start now. The only thing I have signed was a list of personal gifts which my wife brought me in Lubyanka. As soon as I had signed that I had received them, they were taken away. I have no faith in signing things.'

'Speaking as your legal adviser,' says Borovik grandly, 'I would say that it is important for the British Embassy to be sure that you have read these documents.'

'Why? That I have read a lot of cooked-up lies? So what?'

'It is a question of legal procedure,' says Borovik.

'I'm afraid I do not follow you.'

'I advise you very strongly to sign,' he says. 'If you do not trust me, it will be difficult for me to conduct your defence to the best possible advantage.'

I do not trust Borovik because I am sure that he will have no effect whatever on the course of the trial. The only good Borovik has done me, or is ever likely to do me, is to give me a bar of chocolate. But now I am exhausted and I cannot think of any harm in admitting that I have read something, so in the end, after more argument, I write that I have read the documents and that as far as I can tell the translation is accurate, and sign my name.

That is the last I ever hear of the matter. My signature has no value or consequence. That Borovik took so much trouble to obtain it is typical of the farce of Soviet justice.

The Court Session of the Military Collegium of the U.S.S.R. in the case of O. V. Penkovsky and G. M. Wynne began at the Supreme Court of the U.S.S.R. on the 7th May 1963.

On the evening before I am taken to the warden's office. The interpreter is present. The warden is a strict military man. He has never treated me badly, but this evening he is almost jovial. He says tomorrow is the big day, and how am I, and I say I am as fit as a flea, and the warden says it is im-

On trial for their lives. In the dock are Greville Wynne (*above*) and
Oleg Penkovsky (*below*).

*Overleaf* The grim scene in the Moscow court. The dock is in the far
right corner.

# Mementoes of prison life

The author had an English calendar in his cell, on which he ticked off the days of his imprisonment.

A pathetic, home-made Christmas card handed to 'Mister Winn' by a fellow prisoner at Vladimir.

portant for me to look my best in court. Have I any requests, says the warden. I ask for a shower, and some cigarettes and soap from my luggage. These, says the warden, will be permitted. Is there anything else I would care to request? If it had been the Lieutenant-Colonel I would probably have said yes, a free pardon, but as it is my non-enemy warden, I say, in all honesty and not dreaming what is going to happen, I say yes, if it is permitted, I would appreciate some shampoo, so that I may discipline my hair for public appearance. The interpreter is sent off, and when we are alone, the warden, who does not speak English, evidently has something he wishes to tell me. He hums and ha's and then points to his finger where a wedding ring would be, and links arms with me, and nods, rubbing his finger, and waves his hand as if meaning 'out there', and from all this I gather that my wife is going to attend the trial.

I know that the warden is trying to be friendly but it is a terrible way to receive this news, a sudden unexpected stab in the heart.

Now I am taken back to the cell and a few minutes later a guard comes in bringing, to my surprise, to my delight, to my joy (in spite of great despondency at the thought of my trial), the bottle of Tokay wine which in a fit of temper, on my very first evening in Lubyanka, I had described as shampoo.

Because I am not allowed to have the bottle itself (with which, having smashed it, I might do dire things), the guard pours half of it into my prison mug, and when I say that I require all my shampoo he fetches another mug, and then solemnly precedes me down the corridor to the wash-house, where he gives me the two tin mugs of Tokay and remains outside the door, observing me through the spy-hole.

It is clear that some of the precious wine will have to go over my hair, but I am determined that much of it will go down my throat. First I put the mugs on the floor and my clothes on the wooden stool. Then I stand under the rusty rose in the ceiling and find, sure enough, that the water is good and hot. Now I go near the door to dry myself and, while I have still got the towel in my hand, I pick up one of the mugs and pour a few drops of Tokay on to my head, and draping the towel on my shoulder I rub my hair with my free hand. The guard is still watching me through the spy-hole, and now comes the crux. I turn my back on him and raise the towel to my head, and when I calculate that the flapping towel is blocking his view, I take a quick swig of Tokay. I do not know whether the seven months' maturation has made any difference, but I seem to be drinking sugary egg-nog with a kick like brandy. I gasp and splutter and take deep breaths to stop myself choking, but the guard has not noticed any-thing, and from now on it is a pantomime of hair-drops, mas-sage, rub-a-dub, swig, till halfway through the second mugful I have swallowed all the Tokay I want, so I pour the rest over my hair, and drop the towel and the mug, and work my scalp madly with both hands, while the sweet yellow liquid runs down my face and shoulders, and with a last lick as it passes my mouth I wipe up the dregs, have a final shower and get dressed, and the guard lets me out and takes me back for supper. I am allowed a comb, and as I pass the comb through my hair, the guard points and grins and says, 'Koroshi?' which means 'good'. 'Koroshi! Koroshi!' I say, and the guard goes away and I am left alone. I sleep well after my shower and my wine. In the morning I am given a good breakfast.

The trial is due to start at ten o'clock. As we approach the Supreme Court, I see that the diversion has produced a stream of vehicles going round the end of the building. I do not realise (as I later discover) that the traffic has been di-verted chiefly for my benefit.

I am marched under guard through the entrance hall to the courtroom and into the dock. It is a long dock, with Alex at one end and I at the other. Armed guards stand between us, and we have no chance of talking.

The great hall is crammed full with about five hundred citizens, described in the official account of the trial as 'representatives of the workers of Moscow'. Over a hundred are hired applauders who always sit in the front rows. They look an ugly bunch. Their collected faces, greedy with anticipation and hostility, remind me of the crowd at a bullfight. Their duty, as I shall find, is to applaud when the prosecutor makes a point. Somewhere further back my wife is sitting, but I cannot see her. Under a hammer and sickle on the wall the chief officers of court sit on a raised dais. They are the presiding judge, General Lieutenant of Justice; two other generals termed 'people's assessors'; and the Court Secretary, Major of Administrative Service. The two counsel for the defence sit below the dock and with them sit three interpreters. I see at once that they have control knobs on the table, which can only be a bad omen for what I shall say into my microphone. The foreign journalists sit at the far end of the court under open windows, through which already comes the noise of traffic. Even before we begin it is clear that the Press, if they hear anything I say, will only hear what the interpreters decide is good for them. Besides this I find that the leads of my headset have been shortened, so that I am forced to sit with my head down, which will make it almost impossible to convey that I am reading off notes, unless I make some forbidden comment, and furthermore a new shelf for notes has been fixed at a low level.

The whole scene is brutal, spectacular, and has little to do with justice. I remember the tears in Alex's eyes as we left the courtroom in London.

And now the court is called to rise, and the presiding judge declares the session to be open. The Secretary reads a list of witnesses who have been subpoenaed, of experts who are in attendance, and of interpreters. Alex and I in turn are asked to give our birth dates and a brief account of our education and family background. We are asked if we wish to make any petition, as is our right, and we say no. Defence counsel are asked if they wish to petition, and they say no. No one has any petitions. Of what use would petitions be?

Now the Secretary reads the bill of indictment, which begins with the statement that the accused, O. V. Penkovsky, 'as a result of moral degradation, decided to become an agent of the imperialist intelligence services.'[1] Here, at the outset, is the thought that dominates the trial. Everything that follows, the whole labyrinth of question and fact, is designed to prove this point. The question is whether you believe that Alex Penkovsky acted from moral degradation or from the highest form of patriotism. The representatives of the workers of Moscow have one opinion, and I have another, and both our opinions will be confirmed.

The indictment then proceeds to a long and accurate account of most of what Alex had done from the time he first met me to the moment of his arrest, of many of our meetings in Moscow, London and Paris, of the packages and information that Alex gave me. It is a completely damning indictment as far as our actions went, though Alex's true motives and my true position as a knowing agent are obscured and distorted. On the basis of this indictment we are therefore accused as follows:

'Oleg Vladimirovich Penkovsky [details of military career and family] is accused of betraying his Motherland. While on an official trip to London in April–May 1961 he gave a written pledge to collaborate with the British and American Intelligence services and transmitted information constituting a state secret of the Soviet Union. While on trips to London in July–August 1961 and to Paris in September–

1. Written and verbal statements during the trial itself are quoted verbatim from a transcript of the proceedings which was smuggled out of the Soviet Union.

October 1961, he repeatedly met with British and American Intelligence officers at secret apartments, gave them top secret information of an economic, political and military nature, and took training in espionage techniques. During his collaboration with the British and American Intelligence services, including Wynne and others, on the streets of Moscow, in the entrances of buildings, and in hotels, he received instructions of spy equipment, and transmitted secret information orally, in written word and on film.'

There follows:

'Greville Maynard Wynne [details of birth, education, family and business] is accused of having reported, in April 1961, to British Intelligence concerning Penkovsky's proposal to collect and transmit espionage information to the British, and subsequently of having carried out the assignments of British Intelligence to effect communication between the British and American Intelligence services and Penkovsky. During trips of Penkovsky to London and Paris, he met him, received espionage material from him, and transmitted them to British Intelligence officers, and took part in organising secret meetings between Penkovsky and representatives of the British and American Intelligence services. While in Moscow in 1961, he transmitted to a British Intelligence officer packages with espionage information provided by Penkovsky, and delivered to Penkovsky packages with instructions from the intelligence headquarters, photographs of intelligence officers, a Minox camera and film for it, and containers in which Penkovsky could transmit espionage materials.'

'Accused Penkovsky, do you plead guilty as charged?'
'Yes, I plead guilty in all respects.'
'Accused Wynne, do you plead guilty as charged?'
'Yes, I plead guilty, except for certain details about which I shall explain in my depositions.'

There is now a thirty-minute recess and, when the court reassembles, the cross-examination of Penkovsky begins. Just as the prosecutor rises to his feet, I see, wedged far back among the tight-packed crowd, my wife. She is next to a member of the British Embassy staff. Our eyes meet and she raises her hand, but when I start to wave back my hand is slapped down by a guard. It is almost worse to see her sitting there than to see no one. She looks so lost in this huge savage throng of death-thirsty applauders. They have come to see their man condemned to death. That is their pleasure and their expectation. I think of the promise which Alex said was made to spare his life if he confessed in open court. I do not give a straw for this promise.

It is now about eleven o'clock and till two o'clock Alex is cross-examined by the prosecutor. By question and answer the full details of the indictment are drawn out one by one. How Alex and I first met. How he came to London. How he was recruited. The code names of several British agents with whom he and I worked. The packages that were delivered. Now and then I am asked to confirm a place or a time, otherwise it is all Alex and the prosecutor. The name of Alex's defence counsel is Apraksin, but Apraksin has nothing to say during this session. Perhaps he is saving himself for later on, but even this early in the trial it is obvious that the best Apraksin can do will be to mitigate. Refutation is impossible.

Alex conceals all he can, and above all my position as a knowing agent. I know what pressures he had to resist in not telling. I know this from my own experience in Lubyanka, and also from the sight I had of him in his cell and in the interrogation room. They have restored him a little for public appearance. Yet they have not broken him. From the very beginning of the trial he says that it was he, and not I, who made the contact. 'Even before I became acquainted with Mr. Wynne,' he says, 'I began to look for the chance to establish ties with Western Intelligence. Having become acquainted with Mr. Wynne, I decided to try to establish contact with British Intelligence through him. But I did not do this at once. I wanted to study him first in order to discuss this question at subsequent meetings.' Alex is trying to protect me. It will not make much difference, but it is typical of him that he tries.

When it comes to operating procedures, it is clear that the interrogators have not been satisfied with generalities but have insisted on exact and accurate details. Out of many examples, two of the most colourful are the use of the dead-drop box and the method of identification in Moscow. Both of them look like excerpts from a television series, but occasionally real-life Intelligence work does correspond to television.

The indictment had described how, when a dead-drop box is going to be used, Alex had first to paint a black mark on a certain street post, then to put the communication in the hiding place, then to telephone two Moscow numbers and, when the person answered, to hang up.

Now, under cross-examination, he is asked to describe the hiding place. He says:

'It was located on Pushkin Street in the entrance lobby of house number five, between the Meat and Footwear stores, practically opposite the Operetta Theatre. On the right when entering the doorway is a radiator painted dark green. This radiator is fastened with special hooks. Between the radiator and the wall was a gap of approximately six centimetres. I was shown the location of this house on a map of Moscow. It was necessary to place the communication in a matchbox, wrap the box in light blue paper, seal it with cellophane tape, wind wire round it, and hang it on a hook behind the radiator.'

The colour of the radiator, its distance from the wall, and the light blue paper round the matchbox surely make Alex no more guilty than he already is, but the representatives of the workers of Moscow must be shown, no doubt, that nothing escapes the notice of their guardians of justice.

When describing how he made contact in Moscow, Alex says:

'I was to stroll along the Sadovnicheskaya Embankment with a cigarette in my mouth and a book wrapped in white paper in my hand. Obviously the description of my outward appearance was to be known to the one who came to make contact. A man was to walk up to me in an unbuttoned overcoat, also with a cigarette in his mouth, who would say: "Mr. Alex, I am from your two friends, who send you a big, big welcome." The double emphasis of "big, big" and "from your two friends" was agreed upon.'

Here the details are certainly more relevant, but the description gives me a pang, because the same sort of identification was used in Paris, and I remember the sunshine in Paris that September, and how Alex was torn whether to escape to the West then, as he easily could have escaped, or to go back to Moscow with increasing danger, and how he chose to go back, which is why he is standing in the dock now, so bowed and quiet, stared at by the greedy mob in front of him. At the words 'two friends' the mob rumbles with anger. They do not think that this man should have any friends. And a little later, when Alex is explaining a note written by him and found on his person when he was arrested, there is an even bigger outcry. This note was written as a covering letter for some material which Alex intended to give to one of our agents in Moscow, but the opportunity for passing the material did not arise, and Alex felt ill at this time and postponed contacting the agent, and was arrested. The note reads: 'My dear friends . . . I heartily shake your hands. Thank you very much for your concern for me. I will always feel that you are next to me. Your friend. 5th September 1962.' When the mob hears that Alex not only has friends but reckons he is a friend to them, there is a throaty roar such as many a White Russian must have heard in the days of the Revolution.

For three hours Alex is answering the prosecutor's questions, and the crowd growls and roars, and you can feel the hatred and the death-lust steaming up from the packed benches to envelop the man in the dock. He is tired now, his answers come more slowly, and the weaker he gets, the louder become the jeers of the workers. They know he is going to die, but they want him to suffer first.

At two o'clock there is a recess. Alex and I are taken to separate cells in the Supreme Court building. Mine is a cold unlived-in cell. Its walls are a hideous crimson. The tiny shaft of light leaves most of the wall area in a mottled, gory gloom. My lunch sickens me. I feel like Jonah in the whale's stomach.

At four o'clock the afternoon session begins.

After a little more about Paris, there is a long analysis of the instructions Alex received about the positioning of caches in Moscow and how to operate them and when to use them, and now we are in the winter of 1961–2, when Alex had gone back from Paris and was alone in Moscow. I could not get to him because excuses for my being in Moscow had run out, and some new excuse had to be found. This was when the idea of my caravans was conceived, during this winter, but it took months to build them and in the meantime Alex was alone, and a contact for him had to be found. The only contact who could be found was an English woman, the wife of someone who lived in Moscow. I shall tell more about her later, but for the moment all that need be said is that she did her best but was not experienced enough. It was a very difficult and dangerous time, and she could not be blamed for what happened, but it was while Alex was working with her that the observations were made which led finally to his arrest. When I hear Alex being questioned about this period I feel desperately cut off from him, I feel his hopelessness, as

I felt it that winter when I was in England and could not reach him.

Towards the end of this session the prosecutor asks Alex whether he recognises the seriousness of his crimes, and Alex says he fully recognises them. 'And how,' asks the prosecutor, do you explain your crime? What personal qualities in you promoted this?'

There is a long pause, and then Alex begins to speak in a dull monotonous voice which sounds like an old phonograph record played through the lips of a corpse:

'The meanest qualities; moral decay, caused by constant daily use of alcoholic beverages, and dissatisfaction with my position on the Committee. There were also inherited qualities, which were perhaps slow in coming out, but now they undermined me, and in difficult moments I was drawn to alcohol. I lost the road, stumbled at the edge of an abyss, and fell. Vanity, vainglory, dissatisfaction with my work, and the love of an easy life led me to the criminal path. This is all true, but it does not excuse or justify my crime in any way. Morally base qualities and complete corruption—I admit all this. I deceived my comrades and said that everything was well with me, but in fact everything was criminal, in my soul, in my head, and in my actions.'

There is a dead silence. Even the mob makes no sound. It is as if they have been yelling for the man's clothes to be torn off one by one, and now at last, by this final, awful and absolute confession, he stands naked and defenceless and gutted. I could hardly bear to listen to what Alex was saying, because I knew that it was false, that it had been written for him and drilled into him with threats and phoney promises. But it does not help that I know. This is what he has said, and on this he will be judged.

'I have no questions for Penkovsky,' says the prosecutor.

And now, when Alex's trial is as good as over, defence counsel Apraksin jumps up and begins to ask certain mitigating questions, but no one pays much attention, and there is an air of anticlimax in the court. Apraksin asks Alex about his war record, which was very good, and his decorations, and he gives Alex the opportunity of suggesting that on some occasions he met Allied Intelligence people at parties where there was a lot of drinking, as if to imply that alcohol was really the cause of the whole trouble, but the line of questioning is half-hearted, and no one cares. Then Borovik, just to be in the picture, picks up a remark by Alex that on one occasion he had given me a packet and I had seen the contents. Borovik asks me whether it is true that I actually saw the contents, and I have to say no, it wasn't. But this tiny discrepancy will alter nothing for anyone, and after Borovik has established that I may have known the general nature of the material that was passed, but not the particulars, he says that he will postpone further questions to Penkovsky till later.

'The accused Wynne,' says the judge, 'do you have questions for the accused Penkovsky?'

'No,' I answer, 'I have no questions for the accused Penkovsky.'

A recess is declared till ten o'clock tomorrow.

The first day belonged to Alex. The second belonged to me. My cross-examination was long and detailed, but three main points must be borne in mind.

First, the evidence on which Alex and I differed. These small differences were inevitable. Our main plan, in which I was to appear as a businessman, we had prepared; but since we were interrogated for seven months separately and intensively, there were questions which we had not covered and could not have anticipated, and on some of these we had given contradictory answers. These contradictions had been seized on by the interrogators for the purpose of showing in court that I disagreed with Alex and by implication resented his denials of what I said was true. The idea was not to help me in any way or to mitigate the seriousness of what I had done, but simply to show that even this worthless foreigner could not stand the degenerate Penkovsky. When these matters arose, I followed in general the line of my rehearsal. To depart at once from the rehearsal would have meant that the trial would have been transferred to *camera*, nor would it have helped Alex. By obeying the rehearsal I was doing myself a small amount of good, because I was showing that I was prepared to do what I had been told.

The second point is the question of how British Intelligence had employed me. All along I had maintained that at first I knew nothing of my real function, though as time went on I began to get a glimmering of what was happening. It suited the Russians for British Intelligence to appear all-powerful and me to appear as a puppet, and it suited me. This part of the examination came out exactly as London wished, and over one detail, as will be seen, I was able to get away with a false account of how things had been managed.

The third point is my revolt from the script of the rehearsal. As the day went on there were things which even I, with self-preservation at heart, could not stomach. I gave unrehearsed answers, which did me no good. Whether they actually increased the severity of my sentence it is impossible to say, but I am glad I revolted.

The first few minutes of the day are used as a lead-in from Alex to me. Alex says that when he was in London, I used my car to drive him round on his delegation duties, and also that I transmitted his espionage material. I am asked: 'Did you play the part of chauffeur or of someone more important than a chauffeur?' I answer: 'I saw my basic task as helping Penkovsky when he was in London. I understood and realised fully the part I had played in this affair only when I was brought here to Moscow.'

A little later Alex is asked about the fur coat we had seen

in a Moscow store. It will be remembered that under interrogation I had claimed (quite truthfully) that we had
examined furs and asked their prices, but that in the end I
had bought nothing. Now Alex is saying that he had suggested that I used some of the money which he had obtained
from Soviet friends in London to buy a coat for my wife. He
says that I may have postponed my purchase, but that as far
as he knows I did not change my intention. But the whole
suggestion of receiving money from Alex was denied by me
under interrogation, and I deny it again now. I say there was
never any reference to money, and that when I calculated the
Customs duties, I decided I could not afford this fur coat.

'These details are not needed by the court. Accused
Wynne, sit down.'

They do not care about my calculations, they only wish to
show conflict between Alex and me.

Now my examination proper begins, and I am taken
through my various visits to Moscow, my meeting with Alex,
and his visits to London, all of which are accurate in time and
place.

Now comes the question of who it was who first suggested
that I travel to the Soviet Union on business, and it is here
that I am able to mislead the court, because my answers were
foreseen and prepared long ago in London, and I have never
departed from them.

'In one of the business firms for whom I worked,' I say,
'there was a security officer.'

'How did you learn that he was a security officer?'

'I learnt that this man was a security officer by the way I
was first introduced to him.'

'Did he make recommendations to you about your behaviour in the Soviet Union?'

'Yes, he told me I must keep an exact record of my jour-
neys and of the names of Soviet engineers and the firms they
worked for.'

So the picture is built up that the security organisation for which I began to operate was a private affair, and nothing to do with British Intelligence, and that Penkovsky's first approach to me was by enquiring about this security officer, through whom he finally gained access to British Intelligence.

Now I am questioned at length about the hotels where Alex stayed and where he was interrogated. The hotels I have to admit, because they are known and Alex has admitted them. But I stick to the line that I knew nothing about the interrogations and was never present when they took place.

All this comes out as it was rehearsed. For over an hour I have been following my notes. My head is kept down by the shortened leads of the headset, and although I have tried to raise and lower my head to show I am reading off notes, I have not been successful. I am feeling very depressed by this recitation, especially when I see the interpreter at the table below me turning down the volume of my transmission, so that the microphone goes dead sometimes even when I am faithfully following the script and I can see the foreign Pressmen at the far end of the hall moving restlessly because they cannot hear, and casting annoyed glances at the open windows through which comes the roar of traffic. It is now suddenly that my temper flares up and I make an indiscreet answer. I am being questioned about an incident during one of my last visits to Moscow, when I accept a package from a contact in his private apartment. The package is for Alex, and my line is that I had no idea of its contents or true significance. Nevertheless I have admitted that the interview was conducted in silence. 'Then he gestured,' I say, 'and put his finger on his lips, and wrote on a sheet of paper: "Give this to your friend." '

'Why was all this done in silence?'

'Because I had been told that in the next room lived a Russian girl who had been seen in the company of Soviet men, and that it was essential that as few people as possible knew of the negotiations between Penkovsky and certain other persons, otherwise the information about these negotiations might be published in the Press before the matter became official.'

'But there was no representative of the Press in this apartment.'

And here, though it is far from the script, I answer:

'No, but it is no secret to the people in the West that in apartments occupied by foreign residents in Moscow there are very often microphones for listening in.'

The prosecutor is startled by this and very angry. He pauses, looking as if he has something unpleasant in mind, and for an awful moment I wonder whether I have gone too far and whether this will be the end of the hearing in open court. But the presiding judge makes a movement with his hand and chips in with a new question of no importance, and my indiscretion is glossed over.

A few minutes later I am asked whether, during my trips to Moscow, I understood that I was being used by British Intelligence as an intermediary, and here I am only too pleased to follow the rehearsal script, not because it will satisfy the Russians but because the whole substance of my answers was rehearsed long ago in London. I quote the exchanges in court fully. They are a fine example of the prevision with which London made sure that, in the event of my arrest, matters would be described in the way most suitable for British Intelligence.

The prosecutor asks:

'During these trips of yours, you did not understand that you were the intermediary between British Intelligence and Penkovsky?'

'At the time I did not understand, but afterwards I had suspicions, which were confirmed later in England.'

'You mean that at that later period you began to have serious suspicions?'

'Yes, that is so. With your permission I would like to state to the High Court that at the time I actually knew nothing of these matters. My statement may sound naive to the professionals, but I am a businessman, a trader, and I did not know the methods of Intelligence services. Now I understand them.'

The mob laughs at this picture of a dupe, and the prosecutor goes on:

'Tell me, defendant Wynne, how would you evaluate the behaviour of an Englishman, working for the government, who, outside of his country's official channels, would be in secret communication with representatives of another state?'

'It all depends what it is about. If it is a question of state secrets, I would not touch this low dirty affair at any price. But if it is a question of commercial manœuvres, I have been busy with them all my life.'

'Don't you consider that your replies are excessively naive?'

'I am used to trusting people, and I believed that if I could not trust the words of my countrymen, educated people with respectable positions, then whom could I trust? All my conversations with Penkovsky were conducted politely, and I could not subject them to cross-examination, I could not demand proof and so on.'

'But Penkovsky told you straightforwardly what meetings had been held, and what the character of those meetings were?'

'Not at all. He never mentioned such words as "intelligence work", "espionage", "military secrets". He never said anything of this.'

'Defendant Wynne, what business then could British Intelligence have had with Penkovsky except Intelligence?'

'None, of course, but I thought them to be workers of the British ministry of foreign affairs, I thought they were gentlemen, respectable people, worthy of the respect of their countrymen.'

'In short, we may understand you to say that your countrymen deceived you?'

'Exactly so, and it is because of this that I am here now.'

There is more laughter in court, and for once I would like to join in, because this account of me as a poor ignorant businessman is precisely what London had hoped for.

The next significant encounter is over a package which Alex had given me containing a Minox camera for replacement. Alex is now asked in court whether he told me what was inside the package. 'Yes,' says Alex, 'I told him I was handing over a broken camera. Wynne even asked me about the damage to the camera, saying that perhaps I broke it because I did not use it correctly.'

'Defendant Wynne, was there such a conversation between you and Penkovsky?'

In rehearsal I had been made to say that I knew about the camera, but now I answer, 'No, he never explained the contents of the packages.' I say this because Alex has made one of his very few errors in tactics. He should never have said that I knew what was being passed, and the harm coming to him from my denial will be less than the harm to me from admitting that I was a knowing agent.

The incident of the camera took place during my last visit to Moscow in the spring of 1962, and now I am asked:

'Defendant Wynne, did you realise at last that this was a matter of espionage in which you were taking part?'

'Yes, in my own way I now realise that I was mixed up in some dirty business.'

This is the end of the morning session.

The second session begins, after a few preliminary skirmishes, with another demonstration of the all-powerful unscrupulousness of British Intelligence. This protects me, satisfies London, and pleases Moscow. The incident, of course, is untrue. It tells how I was bullied into meeting Alex in Paris when I did not wish to go. The villain is a British agent whom I will call Robbins. He was a charming man who never bullied me at all.

'Defendant Wynne, you have testified that Robbins insisted on your trip to Paris, and even threatened you.'

'Yes, that is true. At the beginning of our discussion, Robbins was very friendly and nice, but when he understood my unwillingness to go to Paris, he began to threaten me and said my business would suffer if I did not help him. Believe me, in England a telephone call to the director of any firm is enough to damage my reputation as a businessman, and I did not want that, since business is my life.'

'Is it correct, then, that you went to meet Penkovsky in Paris under threat from British Intelligence?'

'It is correct. Except—and I must emphasise this—that Robbins stated several times that he was nothing to do with Intelligence, and that my business in Paris would have nothing to do with Intelligence.'

'But how can you say this? You have said in court that Robbins is a member of Intelligence.'

'No, I have said that at the time we are speaking of, Robbins was known to me as an officer of the British security acting under the British Ministry of Foreign Affairs. Robbins clarified his function by telling me that he was responsible for seeing that talks with Penkovsky should not get into the Press and thereby spoil the chances of further talks at a higher level.'

Confusion piled on mystification! Whatever am I talking about? What subtle distinction am I hinting at between security services and Intelligence? It is beyond me, and it is certainly beyond the prosecutor. The matter is dropped.

Instead I am asked a long string of dreary and unimportant questions about the Paris visit, where I stayed and how many times I saw Penkovsky and who paid for the meals and entertainment, and from there we move to my last time in Moscow, and great play is made about a tin of Harpic disinfectant which had a false bottom where fifteen pieces of film could be hidden, another of my methods of taking material to Alex, and then on to some photographs I gave Alex showing four other possible contacts whom he might use in my absence; and all the while I have the feeling that I am on the last stage of questioning, and that the prosecutor is harbouring and nurturing his resentment at my several earlier lapses from the script, and that sooner or later he is going to ask me some vital and final question, to which all these details have been building up. Of course this is more than a feeling, because although there is plenty of *ad lib*. cross-examination, I have been rehearsed in the outlines, and I know at the back of my mind that something is coming, but I am so tired after six hours in the dock that I forget what this something is, and I have no time to look ahead in the notes. But at six o'clock there is a short recess, and I remember what question I shall have to answer. It is when I am asked what I think of my actions in the Union, and I am supposed to say that I am very sorry and bitterly repent my actions and the crimes I committed because I have always found in the Soviet Union only 'friendship and hospitality and peaceful co-existence'.

Sitting in my red cell, I know that I shall never be able to utter such a lie, no matter what my refusal may incur. There will be no sense in being downright rude at this point, but I know that the slightest departure from the script will be very unpopular, because a full-blooded repentance has been insisted on and drilled into me during rehearsal.

When the court reassembles there is a flutter in my stomach, and I look across at my wife, but she is hidden for the moment behind a large worker. The prosecutor takes me through a short passage where I have to say that back in

England in the summer of 1962 I 'crossed swords' with British Intelligence and told them I could not stand their 'lies', and then he says:

'After you crossed swords with Intelligence and read them a moral about their lies, did they repent?'

'No,' I say, 'they never repent.'

'And how do you evaluate now all your criminal actions against the Soviet Union?'

Here is my cue for repentance. I take a short breath and cough into the microphone, which I can tell is fully amplified. I say clearly: 'Well, I have no intention of coming to the Soviet Union and abusing the goodwill shown to me by the Ministry of Foreign Trade.'

This is no more than the truth, because in this narrow sphere I have been welcome, but it leaves out the eulogy about Soviet life in general. The prosecutor is furious. He gives me further cues. How do I feel about my activities? What statements have I to make? But I answer shortly that I did not ask to get involved in espionage and when I became involved, I did not like it. Finally the prosecutor snarls, 'Do you then disapprove of your actions?' and when I simply answer, 'Yes, I definitely disapprove,' he sits down with a grim face, and Borovik gets up to ask some tame questions about my active service career in the war, and is it not true that I came to Moscow in good faith to bring a delegation of businessmen, and will I please repeat my evidence that as time went on I felt the ever tightening 'vice' of British Intelligence.

These mitigations make no impact on the bench of judges, who are clearly still thinking of my failure to repent. During the early part of my examination they looked thoughtful and interested, they would glance at me as if trying to form an opinion, and when the interpreter spoke they would lean forward intently. But now they are sitting like cold rocks. There is a nasty indifference on the bench, and after two expert witnesses have been called to testify about a faked passport found in Alex's apartment and a typewriter and some paper capable of taking secret writing, and other experts have been instructed to report in due course about the Minox camera and the radio receivers used by Alex, the evening session comes to an end.

The last words of the day are spoken by the Court Secretary who says:

'The next session of the Military Board will be tomorrow, *in camera,* at 10 a.m.'

Well, I asked for it, and now I have got it. I do not know how far I have damaged my case, and I do not much care. I am exhausted. I have had my day in open court, and maybe the foreign Press will draw their own conclusions from the signs and the tones of voice I have tried to get through to them, and from the regulated microphone and the din of traffic. Something may have been achieved, a few sparks of truth for the outside world, but as far as my own case goes, nothing will be altered. My sentence was, I am sure, decided long before the court convened. As I stand up to be marched out, I try to catch a glimpse of my wife, but she is hidden in the mob. There is nothing left but to go back to Lubyanka and wait for tomorrow.

But I am wrong. For instead of returning at once to Lubyanka, I am taken to the red cell. It is dark outside, and in the ceiling there is only one small light bulb which makes the top part of the walls appear to be on fire, the crimson glow welling up from the murky floor. I am visited by my detested enemy, the Lieutenant-Colonel, who storms in with the interpreter and two guards. How dare I disobey orders? Do I hope to escape punishment? I am raved at and screamed at and called every kind of criminal, I am reminded of all my stubbornness during interrogation, I am told that the only result of my folly will be an increase of sentence, I am threatened with dark unnamed punishments after the sentence. 'Up to now we have been very patient,' shouts the Lieutenant-Colonel. 'We have merely questioned you. But now you are going to be punished. You will see what happens to you, you will see!'

It is with these words ringing in my ears that I am taken back to Lubyanka.

The third day of the trial is not so much an anticlimax as an almost complete blank. When I am taken into court there are only the officials present, there are no Press and no representatives of the workers of Moscow. A Russian witness whom I have never seen is questioned about the nature of the information passed by Penkovsky, and for a few minutes the interpreter repeats the evidence in English, but before I have got the hang of what is happening, the interpreter is ordered to stand down, and a little later, after listening to the proceedings in Russian, of which I do not follow a word, I am taken out of court. The transcript of the trial states that 'the court questioned witnesses Dolgikh and Petrochenko. Reports were also heard from experts on the degree of secrecy of the information collected and transmitted to foreign Intelligence services,' but at the time, in my cell, all I know is that the court is free to proceed without comment or report from the Press, and I wonder whether my absence will damage my case. I know that it will not, because I am sufficiently damaged as it is, but I cannot help wondering.

So the last day comes, and I am keyed up to answer any questions as stoutly as I can. But I need not have worried, because the only questions I am asked all morning are about my expenses in Paris, and I answer that British Intelligence paid only the expenses incurred in my meetings with Penkovsky, the other business expenses being paid by the firm I was representing.

'You received no additional money for payments for yourself personally?'

'No, I received no material reward; on the contrary, I paid all kinds of minor expenses out of my own pocket.'

This is true, but it will not, I am afraid, affect my sentence.

The rest of the morning session is taken up with examination of two witnesses named Rudovsky and Finkelshteyn, men who had known Alex socially and are being questioned to establish the sort of life he lived in Moscow. Of the two, I prefer Rudovsky who seems to me to avoid saying anything more than is dragged out of him. No, he cannot recall very much what Penkovsky used to talk about. He cannot remember accurately what Penkovsky's interests were. They talked about everyday matters, never about Penkovsky's work. The only answer that may be damaging is when the prosecutor, after establishing that Penkovsky had known a girl named Galya, asks, 'Witness Rudovsky, were there any evenings or other meetings when the slippers of Penkovsky's beloved were used as goblets?' and Rudovsky answers, 'One time I was with Penkovsky and his lady friend at the Poplavok restaurant in the Park of Culture. I had no woman with me and did not drink from the slipper. I don't know if it was to show his love for the girl, or because it was a Western practice, but Penkovsky poured wine into the slipper and drank it.'

There is a slight sensation in court (shared by myself, I must confess, in an Edwardian sort of way) at the thought of decadent Westerners quaffing their wine from slippers, but I doubt whether even this extravagance can add very much to the Soviet conviction of Alex's moral degeneracy.

The witness Finkelshteyn, on the other hand, seems anxious to tell how much time Penkovsky spent at football games and theatres and movies and restaurants, and how wide was his circle of women friends, and how lavish he was with presents for everyone. Temperamentally, says Finkelshteyn, Penkovsky was secretive, vain and obstinate; he read few books, or if he did read, then only popular best-sellers and never a book of culture, and yes, it was true about drinking wine from the girl's slipper, Finkelshteyn had also witnessed that, and on the same evening Penkovsky was showing attention to another woman, the wife of one of his friends. All in all, where Rudovsky tried to say a little less than was asked, Finkelshteyn tries to say a little more. Finkelshteyn, in my view, is a louse.

Now the expert who was asked to examine the radio receivers gives a long report describing the sets in detail and stating that they were capable of receiving long-range transmissions, and after this a deposition is read from a witness named Kasantsev who is absent through illness. Kasantsev was a member of the Soviet delegation to London. He describes how Penkovsky prolonged the visit, and how Penkovsky was the sole arranger of everything, and how Penkovsky was often absent on unexplained business, and how, at lunch in the north of England one day, Penkovsky was overcome with a stomach complaint, from which he recovered some three hours later! How well I remember that day.

And now, after the few short questions about my expenses, there is a recess till four o'clock.

The afternoon session is taken up with four long speeches, two by the prosecutor who is making his final arraignment first against Alex and then against me; one by Apraksin defending Alex, and one by Borovik defending me. The prosecutor speaks in a loud monotonous voice, reciting the accusations against Alex which we have heard so many times, ending with a sermon on Alex's moral degeneracy based on the text: 'I fell into an abyss and became a scoundrel.' The prosecutor's accusations against me are a similar recitation, but without a sermon at the end.

Apraksin's defence of Penkovsky rests on the strange thesis that Penkovsky is not a criminal (though he has performed criminal actions), but a Philistine. A Philistine, defines Apraksin, is someone who is 'oblivious of the basic principle of communist morality—devotion to the Motherland.' So Penkovsky has acted more from ignorance than from evil intent. 'Mistakes and pitfalls,' says Apraksin, 'occur in the life of every man. But the open repentance of this man, his desire to expiate his guilt, and the good that he did in his irreproachable past—all that, despite the depths to which he fell, prove the basis for our request for mercy. I beg you to allow Penkovsky to live! '

Now Borovik takes the floor on my behalf, and although I have every reason to be interested, I somehow cannot fully attend to what is being said, partly because it is evident that his eloquence is falling on stony ears. Borovik begins by saying that his aim is mitigation, and then goes on at length about my visits to Moscow on business, and how gradually and unwittingly I was drawn into becoming a courier, how I never knew what the packages contained, how I was never present when Penkovsky met Intelligence officers in the West, how I fought the good fight in the war, and at long last Borovik begs the Comrade Judges that 'when you are in the deliberation room you will analyse everything, that you will weigh and reweigh all the extenuating circumstances and bring out a just and humane sentence'.

The prosecutor now petitions that, since part of the evidence has been heard in closed session, the final pleas by Penkovsky and Wynne shall likewise take place in closed session. The judge agrees to this, and the court is dismissed.

Today, 11th May 1963, is the day of reckoning. Now all that I have done since that morning in 1956 when my telephone rang heralding the voice of James, and all that Alex has done since years earlier, will be brought to judgement. First we must make our final pleas.

The courtroom seems very big and empty. Alex stands in the dock and begins to speak, and the interpreter translates softly for my benefit. I can see that Alex is taut and strained.

All the resistance, all the evasions, all the arguments are over now. He is pleading for his life.

'Comrade Judge,' he says, 'you have listened patiently to my trial. I ask you to remember that I have given service to the Soviet Union. I was a soldier, a loyal serviceman, and I ask you to be patient. I give my plea for your consideration before you pass sentence. I ask you to . . .'

Suddenly Alex stops. His hands clenched tight. He speaks to the judge, and Borovik turns to me and says that Penkovsky has asked that I should not be present while he makes his plea, and would I object to leaving the courtroom. A guard takes me to a small cell leading out of the courtroom itself. The cell window is shut and when I point to it, the guard shakes his head. I make signs that I shall stifle if I am shut in here, and the guard opens a shutter in the cell door. Now I am locked in, and through the shutter I can hear Alex speaking for his life. He speaks for a long time.

At last I am led into court. Alex is gone, and it is my turn to speak.

I do not say much. I feel more like pleading for Alex than for myself. My head is full of Alex in his strength and health, and my ears are full of his voice. He is going to die, I am sure of this, unless perhaps . . . but there is no perhaps. It is all useless. I say that I have nothing to add to what has been said in court. My speech was prepared by Borovik. I say that I hope I will not have to stay too long in prison. I say that if the court will bear in mind that today, the day of my sentence, is my son's birthday, I will be grateful. I ask for mitigation, that is all.

There is a recess for three or four hours, while the judges decide their verdict, and when we reassemble the courtroom is packed. I look for my wife but I cannot see her. The workers who have come to applaud the sentence are jammed tight together. They have been the same lot every day. I recognise many of their faces. In the front row there has

always been a hideous woman with a red scarf. But today at
least a hundred extra workers have been allowed in for the
great moment.

The sentence in the name of the Union of Soviet Socialist
Republics, read by the presiding judge, begins with yet another short account of the joint crimes committed by the two
defendants, and ends with the findings of the Military Board
of the Supreme Court of the U.S.S.R.:

'Oleg Vladimirovich Penkovsky, guilty of treason to the
Motherland, to be shot to death and all his personal property
to be confiscated.

'Greville Maynard Wynne, guilty of espionage, to be de-
prived of his liberty for eight years, the first three years to be
served in prison, those subsequent to be served in a harsh-
regime correctional labour colony.'

When Alex is sentenced the crowd jeers and claps, while
Alex stands erect and motionless facing them. When I am
sentenced there is a murmur of approval but the clapping is
less. It is not for my punishment that the representatives of
the workers of Moscow have been waiting.

Alex is taken out of court and I never see him again.

I am taken to an ante-room, and my wife is brought in, and
we are told we may have one hour. We embrace, and for a
few moments it seems wonderful to be together, but when
we sit down there is a silence and we do not know what to say.
What is there to say? She tells me that she was not in court
for the sentence. Her escort from the British Embassy advised her not to go in because of the crowd, but she heard
the sentence relayed through loudspeakers in the entrance
hall. She makes no comment, she does not try to cheer me
up, and I am grateful for her wisdom. What is ahead for
both of us, for her as well as for me, is too big, too terrible to
be expressed. There is no remedy. So we talk about small
things. She tells me that when the Embassy car collected her
at the airport they were followed by a Soviet car, and she

was frightened and wondered whether something was wrong, but the Soviet car was chasing them to deliver her luggage which had been left on the pavement. We talk about our friends, and especially about Andrew. But even here, though I want to be told everything possible, I cannot bear to be told too much. It is too painful. I look at the clock on the wall to see how the time is going, but the clock has stopped. I point, but the guard shrugs. Sheila does not show me her watch, she just strokes my hand and smiles. It is not uncommon for Moscow clocks to stop, but this stoppage seems symbolic. Our life has stopped and it will only start again in some unimaginably distant future.

When the time comes for me to go, I dare not kiss her. I lay my cheek against hers, and look into her eyes for a long last moment, then I am gone.

I am taken back to Lubyanka where I stay alone for ten days. No visitors, no interrogations. Mostly I think of Alex. I feel that he is still alive. I feel that he could not have died without my knowing it. I keep going back to the turning point in his story, the time when we were together in Paris and he had the chance of escape to the West. It was his last chance, and we both knew this, but he did not take it.

## II

The Soviet Trade Fair was due to open in Paris in the first week of September 1961. In August I was on holiday in Switzerland, and from there I went to Amsterdam to pick up some material for Alex, and then to Moscow for four days on the pretext of seeing the French Exhibition. Like Alex when he walked through the English Customs, I walked through the Soviet Customs with two large suitcases. With Alex as my pilot, the cases were not opened. This was as well, for they contained a radio receiver and a cluster of paintings whose frames had secret crevices stuffed with unexposed film and operating procedures typed on wafer-thin paper. So little space was left in the cases for travelling gear that Alex had to empty them in his apartment and fill them with enough clothes and accessories to make a showing for the chambermaid at my hotel.

Alex and I did not see much of each other this time. He brought his wife and daughter Galina to meet me for a few minutes because I had a set of English-Russian language records for Galina. She was a lively girl of about fifteen, dark and sturdy, with her father's deep-set intelligent eyes. She was very pleased with the records, and afterwards, when Alex and I were alone for lunch together, he talked about her and I could see he was a proud father.

Apart from this, we hardly met, since it was important not to suggest that he was my only reason for going to Moscow, and anyhow we would probably be meeting in Paris. It was probable that he would come but not certain. If he came his duty would be to make contact with as many French industrialists as possible. He had already led a successful delegation to London, and had been sent to attend the Soviet Exhibition at Earls Court and to accompany Madame Serov. He had established himself as a useful and popular liaison man with the West, especially with me. Moscow had given me an open invitation to the Paris Fair, and it was reasonable to expect that they would wish Alex to keep in touch with the bourgeois contact who had enabled them to arrange the visit to London and who could now give similar help in Paris.

The date of Alex's arrival could not be found out in advance. If he showed too much interest by enquiring, suspicions might be aroused. He might come early or late. I was told to be in Paris by the 6th September and to make sure that I met him at the airport. How I achieved this was my concern. I was to put him in touch as soon as it was safe with other Allied agents, and to be ready at all times to help with the arrangements for transferring him without being observed to an interrogation room which would be set up in a fashionable quarter of Paris.

I had no other special briefing, but before leaving England I was sent on one strange errand whose purpose was not explained till it was over. 'Take this key,' they said. 'Go to the locker section at Victoria Station. Pick up the suitcase from the numbered locker. Carry the suitcase on a circuit of the station, pausing for two minutes to study the Continental timetable board, and again outside the News Theatre. Then walk through to the taxi rank and bring the suitcase here.'

I did as I was told. The suitcase was brand new and had a canvas cover. It felt almost empty, but perhaps there were papers inside. I wondered what precious and significant material I was carrying round Victoria Station. I spoke to no one and no one spoke to me. When I climbed into the taxi I was anxious to know what task I had performed. When I delivered the suitcase I found out. Twenty-four British agents dotted about Victoria, most of them unknown to each other, had been taking a good look at me so that they would recognise me in Paris, where their duties would be partly my protection and partly the organisation of the routes along which Alex could be smuggled to the interrogation room.

On the 6th September I arrived at Le Bourget, and having checked in at my hotel went back to the airport to await the Soviet flight from Moscow. Alex did not appear. From now on I met every Soviet flight. There were one or two each day, except on Saturdays and Sundays when there were none, so that I was able to go home at the weekends, flying back to Paris on Mondays in time for the first Russian arrival. It was not till the 20th September that Alex came smiling through Customs, full of bounce and confidence, for his first visit to the city of gaiety and love. He seemed all set for both. As we drove to his hotel near the Soviet Embassy, his eyes were shining and he slapped my thigh: 'Greville, this is great, really great! Paris, here we come!'

'It won't exactly be all parties,' I smiled. 'You have a few other things to do.'

'Don't worry. There's time for everything. I'm going to eat everything, drink everything, see everything, do everything. Look at that blonde!'

'Already?' I said.

'Sure, why not? The sooner the better.'

A gendarme held us up and Alex turned to look back at the blonde on the pavement.

'Paris is full of girls,' I said, 'but you've got to behave. No stray contacts.'

'I suppose you've no objection if I look around at the Embassy or the Exhibition?'

'That's better. But be careful.'

'Yes, sir. I'll be careful. I'll find a nice little girl from Moscow.'

'We've got some nice girls from London, all laid on.'

'The more the merrier,' said Alex happily.

When I thought of what was ahead for him, the long days of talking to French industrialists and engineers, the long evenings of Soviet Embassy functions, the long nights of interrogation, and, on top of all this, the evidently monumental amours he had in mind, I could only admire the belief in his own energy. But this was Alex. He was ready for everything, and he looked it. At the hotel he handed over fifteen rolls of film and a mass of photographed documents, and declared, 'Now we are all set for business!'

The first couple of days he spent settling in, meeting the Embassy officials, and sightseeing with me. We went everywhere. Up the Eiffel Tower, round and round the Louvre, down the Seine in a *bateau-mouche*. German girls with Leicas, American girls with expensive movie cameras, French girls with smiles, Alex flirting madly but at last restraining himself from making dates with unknown beauties. Such rendezvous were strongly discouraged. To the Arc de Triomphe, to the Invalides, to the Flea Market. Down the Champs Élysées, up the Capucines. 'Come on, Greville, no taxis, you're not tired yet.' Never had we been so free to meet. Alex was positively encouraged to spend time with me, since it was I who could best arrange his meetings with French businessmen. When I disclosed a stiff programme of office meetings and visits to factories, he brushed it aside: 'That's fine, Greville, we'll soon deal with these.' And he was as good as his word. His vitality suited the French, and wherever he went he was welcomed and loaded with catalogues, brochures and information. One visit in particular earned him applause in Moscow. A factory making silicon transistors had been visited some time before by Khrushchev himself, but even Khrushchev had not been shown one special feature, the de-dusting chamber through which workers had to pass before going to the benches where particles shaken from their clothes might damage the delicate wiring on which they were engaged. The floor of the chamber was laid with a tacky substance for picking up dirt from the soles of shoes. The walls were fitted with vast suction pipes and, when the door was closed and the motors were turned on, the man in the chamber had a cord round his waist to stop the jacket being sucked off his back. His trousers billowed, his jacket bulged, his tie flapped towards the wall, and when he came out every shred of dust had been vacuumed away. Khrushchev did not see this but Alex saw it and his report duly reached the Kremlin files.

It was a wonderful autumn. As we marched down the boulevards the delightful Parisians, back from their summer holidays, sipped their morning coffee at the pavement tables, there was a balmy fragrance in the air, the shops glittered with their new displays, and even the hee-haw of the police vans sounded cheerful. In the early evening the cafés of the

Champs Élysées were crowded with office workers taking a beer or an aperitif on their way home. We sat with our lager and saw the Arc de Triomphe bathed in a fiery sunset, as Paris got ready for an evening of laziness and love. Alex had never seen so many girls in all his life. 'This is better than London,' he said. 'The girls in London are as beautiful, perhaps, but here there are more of them.' There is nowhere in the world more expectant than the Champs Élysées at six o'clock on a September evening. We sat for a few moments watching the strolling crowds, the men with the girls. At a cinema across the road a spy film was showing, and couples were moving up to the box office and vanishing inside for their hour or two of excitement. Alex pointed and smiled:

'Maybe we could learn something, Greville.'

'I shouldn't wonder.'

'One thing you can be sure of. It will all end happily.'

'He'll get the girl, I expect.'

'I was thinking more of the man himself.'

I did not answer this. I knew what he was thinking. Presently he said:

'I don't have to go back. I could stay in the West.'

'I know that.'

'Your people have said I can stay, any time I want. They say they would like more from me, but they don't expect it, they don't demand it. They are quite prepared to set me up in London or New York and look after me. It's entirely up to me. So—what do you say? What's your opinion?'

I shook my head: 'I don't know, Alex. It's up to you.'

'But tell me what you think. I want to know.'

'I don't think anything, it's something you must decide for yourself.'

It was true that I did not know the answer, but apart from not knowing, I had been told by London that if ever Alex talked to me about this problem, I was not to influence him one way or the other.

'There's the question of the work,' he said quietly, as if he were talking to himself, 'and there's the question of my wife and daughter. Tell me, what did you think of Galina? How did she strike you?'

'She's a great girl,' I said, 'and you're very proud of her.'

'I'm more than proud, I am mad about her, I really am. Can you believe that?'

'Why not? It's very natural.'

He gave an accusing little laugh: 'So I suppose you think I'm a pretty fair bastard.'

'I don't think anything of the sort. Why should I?'

'Because instead of being a good father and husband I'm chasing around. I can't help it. But it's still true that I love Vera and Galina, I love them very much. Sometimes I have a sort of dream, that I am just a simple army officer with a nice family waiting at home, and everything is easy and pleasant. That was how it used to be years ago. But not any more. If I stay here it will mean leaving Vera and Galina behind. I can't get them out with me, it's impossible. And if they stayed they would be used to get me back. It would be very bad for them. And yet, you know . . .' He paused and made a hopeless gesture with his hand. '. . . if I go back, it won't really be for them, it will be for myself, for what I have to do. I've been taken over, that's what happened. I'm not just a husband and father any more, I'm something else as well. I'm really two people, can you understand that?'

'Yes,' I said, 'I understand.'

'If we could be like all those people. If we could go back to the beginning. I wonder what would happen.'

'It would be the same over again. You know that.'

I was wondering what else to say, how I could help to relieve the enormous strain in his mind, when I saw he was not paying attention. A blonde girl had sat down at the next table. She was young and *chic* and very invitatious, with a soft mouth and big dark eyes like stains on her pale skin. She was looking straight at Alex and her smile was an unfettered promise. The tension had died out of his face, and he stared at her and said in a far-off voice: 'Greville, isn't there somewhere we could meet up, say in a couple of hours?'

'No,' I said firmly. 'That's out. Forget it.'

Alex looked miserable and shook his head at the girl, and she shrugged and beckoned a paper vendor from the pavement.

Dusk was coming in the east, but the Arc still glowed in the sunset. The air was heavy and warm and no one seemed in a hurry. The café was full, and we watched the people for a while and had another beer. Then we went for dinner to a place in Rue Lincoln where the steak was superb, and after a long meal with wine and brandy even Alex said he would not mind one night's rest. He would not get many from now on. Tomorrow night he was due at the interrogation room. I was to pick him up at a quarter to twelve at a café near his hotel.

There is something about Paris especially suitable for intrigue. So many courtyards with dark doors and alleyways to another street, so many bars and cafés with double exits, so many places to dodge into, such throngs in narrow markets where a follower may be lost, such a babel of European tongues, such a general atmosphere of old-fashioned decay and secrecy (I am speaking, of course, of the days before de Gaulle's ruthless application of paint). The very appearance of a Paris taxi suggests assignation, and the reckless swerving drivers seem bent on dark delivery or vital escape. But above all it is the people themselves. They look born intriguers. To me, at any rate, every Frenchman is up to something. Perhaps I have read too much Maigret.

A personal fancy maybe, but for Alex and me that autumn fancy became fact. Dozens of agents had converged on Paris. The Russians were watching their own nationals at the Trade

Fair, the British and Americans were watching the Russians, and the French were watching everybody. No one knew exactly what they were looking for, and most of the agents did not know one another. As far as I was concerned, everything depended on getting Alex to The Room without being observed. A single slip would end his career as an agent.

The routes were complicated and varied each day. Every morning I was rehearsed on the route for that night. I had to wear the same suit as I had worn at Victoria Station, only my shirt and tie could vary. Each day I used a different car, whose identity was known to my colleagues.

The Room was at the top of a tall house in a fashionable crescent. The garage was attached to the house. An electronic beam raised the shutter as you approached and closed it behind you. At the far end of the garage was another shutter, so that when leaving you could either back out or drive on past the garden into another road. From the garage a lift took you up to The Room. It measured forty feet by twenty and was splendidly equipped with recorders, duplicators, typewriters, projectors, radio to London and Washington, a complete filing system, and an army of interrogators, interpreters, technicians, stenographers and doctors.

The crescent had been chosen because it was not a main thoroughfare, so that late at night the only likely cars would belong to residents and all these cars were known to our agents. From the pavement outside the house you could see both ends of the crescent, but the ends were not visible to each other. This question of vista was really the basis of the whole operation. If Alex were being followed, he must never go near the house, and the best way to spot a follower was to have a long unobstructed view in a preferably unfrequented street.

The beginning of the journey was difficult, for no matter where I picked him up, we could not be certain who might be watching us. Our first step was to have four separate rendez-

vous. At Alex's hotel, at the Exhibition, at a café near the
hotel, and at a café near the Exhibition. Even these four we
varied, not keeping to a strict rotation, but it was still possible that one of the Soviet agents, on a different assignment
perhaps, would observe us and follow.

The next stage was to get into the car and begin our long
circuitous route to the house in the crescent. Sometimes I
took him all the way, and at various vantage points someone
would be waiting to let us know if there were a car behind us.
Our spotter might be a man or a girl. At the Place de l'Étoile,
perhaps, we would drive round twice, and on the second circuit the man would raise his hat or the girl would draw a
scarf over her head if we appeared to have no follower. Sometimes we made for the Place de la Concorde, crossed the river
to the left bank, and came back by one of the other bridges.
Late at night the bridges gave good vistas. Sometimes we
would go up to Montmartre where the narrow streets made
a tracking car more obvious. The man changes his folded
coat from one arm to the other, the girl opens her green
handbag and takes out her mirror. The most dangerous part
of our twisting journey was when, after our long ramble, we
came near to the house. There was no escaping it. Sooner or
later, no matter from which direction we had approached,
we had to turn into the crescent, and having turned in, we
always drew up behind a certain car (which varied every
night) to make sure that no observers on foot were lurking.
In the back of the car ahead sat a man and a girl. If they
started cuddling we were safe to drive on into the garage. If
they kept apart we drove on and made another circuit or
took Alex back to his hotel.

Sometimes I would drop Alex on one side of a bridge and
he would walk across to where another car waited. When he
got out of my car he must never hurry, he must sit and chat
for a few moments, then open the door slowly and stroll
across the bridge. At the far side, if the man continued read-

ing his paper on the embankment, Alex was free to enter the waiting car. If the paper was folded up and put away, he must stroll on. Sometimes the spotters could not be sure whether some loiterer was around by accident or intention, but if there was the slightest doubt the danger signal was made. Alex was in Paris for three weeks, and only on two occasions were we even delayed in reaching the house. We never failed to get there.

These nightly exercises awoke all the alertness of my early training. In the daytime, when my rehearsal was over, I was free to do what I pleased. As I was up to no mischief, it would not have mattered if I had been followed, but from habit I was always on the look-out for anyone who appeared interested in my behaviour. One day, as I left the restaurant after lunch, I paused for a moment on the pavement and caught sight of a man standing some yards away beside a newspaper kiosk. Our eyes only met for a second, but I had the feeling he was watching me. He wore a black beret and looked more like a Frenchman than a Russian, but appearances could never be trusted, so as I had nothing special to do I decided to test his reactions. As I turned away I saw that he started to walk slowly after me.

A little way along the boulevard was a men's clothes shop. I stopped to inspect the cardigans and the man passed behind me and stopped to gaze into the next shop window. I walked on, crossed the road, and headed up towards the Opéra. I was still being followed. I could safely have taken a taxi back to my hotel, he would have gained nothing by finding out where this was, because it was no secret. But I was curious. He looked an unsavoury character, fat, badly dressed, and unshaven. Perhaps he was a Russian after all, there was something about his eyes. It nettled me to think of being trailed by such an oaf. At the next small side street I turned in quickly, walked a few paces to a record shop, and wheeled round. The man was ambling towards me. As he

came near I stared at his face, expecting him to drop his eyes
and pass on. Instead he came up to me with a greasy smile,
thrust his hand into his trouser pocket, and murmured:

'You like some nice pictures, mister?'

Alex's first visit to the crescent was a great success. I did
not stay for the interrogation, but they told me afterwards
that he had been on top form and that it was after four in the
morning when he left. The next day was Saturday, and after
a heavy social programme at the Soviet Embassy his evening
was free. He announced that he had found a girl at the Embassy called Sonja, and that we would be taking Sonja out to
dinner. When I suggested bringing along another girl, he said
no, if I didn't mind, let it just be the three of us because Sonja
did not speak much English and she was rather shy and would
feel out of it if we were all chattering away. 'Besides,' he
added with his charming smile, 'it will be easier for us to slip
away afterwards.'

'Where do you think you are going to slip to?'

'Don't worry, we'll find somewhere.'

'But I do worry, that's my job.' We were talking in my car
on our way to the crescent. The man at the end of the Pont
Alexander III took off his hat and rubbed his hair, and we
drove on.

'Some job,' said Alex. 'The trouble is, you want to supervise my love life.'

'You know the form.'

'Sure. But have a heart. It's Saturday night after all.'

'If you want to talk politics with Sonja in private, you'd
better use the apartment.'

'What apartment?'

I told him. At a hotel near the Madeleine a whole floor had
been taken over by our people, and the best suite reserved
for private entertainment. It was not especially for Alex, but
I said I thought I could fix it.

'Well, you do that, Greville. And you won't mind leaving us alone to talk politics?'

'Not at all.'

'And there's another thing,' said Alex casually. 'What were you saying earlier on about girls from London?'

'Oh, that was nothing important. You won't be wanting other girls now you've got Sonja.'

'No, of course not.' Silence. 'Sonja's very busy, you know. She can't always get away. And besides, she's finding this French food pretty rich. She might not be feeling well one evening.'

'Well, if that happens, you might have to put up with one of the others.'

'Yes, but who *are* they, damn you?'

'They're just some English girls who happen to be over here. They know the city well, and we thought you might like a girl guide now and then, but that was before we knew about Sonja.'

'It was a nice thought anyway,' said Alex.

I had not told quite the truth about the English girls. They did not just happen to be in Paris. We had brought them. They had been carefully selected for their quality as good companions, their expense accounts were generous, and their sole duty was to look after the gentleman from Belgrade should he become lonely. Alex must be kept happy, but it was far too dangerous to allow him to pick and choose for himself. As a trained agent he knew this quite well, but it was better left unsaid, the illusion would be spoilt by explanation.

The next evening I met Sonja. She came to Alex's hotel and we took her to the Champs Élysées because Alex wanted her to see the sunset and the crowds. I do not know what I expected, but Sonja gave me a surprise. She was in her early twenties, attractive, with jet-black hair and an ivory skin, but there was something strangely old-fashioned about her. I knew that Muscovite girls were way behind the Parisiennes in smartness, but it was not only the plain hair style and the simple green dress which looked as if it were home-made. She had a beautifully developed figure, but there was a child-like innocence in her face that I had not seen in the West for many years, and also a naive kind of strength. She made you feel that she meant exactly what she said and that if she made a promise she would be sure to keep it. When she smiled her eyes sparkled, but when she was not smiling they held a look of hopeful enquiry, like your twelve-year-old niece waiting for you to amuse her.

We went to the same café as before. Alex and I drank lager and Sonja drank grenadine. I was introduced, of course, simply as a business friend, and she wanted to know about London, whether it was as big as Paris and what the ballet was like. She could not speak much English, but as long as you spoke slowly she understood very well. Alex had given her a string of amber beads and she was very pleased with the beads and her fingers kept wandering up to touch them, as if to make sure they were still there. She tried hard to join in the conversation but after a while she missed what we were saying and spoke to Alex in Russian, and Alex said sternly, 'No, you must speak English, my girl,' and she said to me with a big smile, 'Sorree, I spik English now always,' and I said, 'I wish my Russian was as good as your English.' It was all very friendly and we got on fine together. Alex was in high spirits and kept pointing things out and saying how wonderful Paris was, and sometimes she would glance at him with an almost frightening devotion.

For dinner we took the Métro to Montmartre. This was their first ride in the Métro and they were delighted with the slow clanking carriage, and Alex read the station names off the map in his deep rich voice. Madeleine, Saint Lazare, Trinité, Lorette, Saint Georges, Pigalle! What music!

We dined at the Restaurant Pigalle where the floor is higher than the pavement and the window space has no glass.

From our side table we could almost touch the heads of the passers by. It was a happy strolling crowd with a good sprinkling of Africans, black girls hand in hand with a Parisian or French girls clinging to a handsome Negro. The strip-tease lights were flashing across the square and the restaurant was noisy and gay. The only two people who appeared not to be enjoying themselves were a pair of elderly overweight Americans at the next table. When they heard us speaking English they volunteered in loud confident voices the absorbing information that they were brothers, that they owned a tyre factory in Detroit, that they were worth between them five million dollars, and that back home the 'blacks' would be cleaning their shoes, not walking about the street as if they were as good as anyone else. The Detroit accent was too much for Sonja and Alex gave her a quick translation. The effect was remarkable. She raised her head, the smile died, and she stared at the brothers as if they were monsters from outer space. A hot blast of Russian spat from her curved lips and the scorn in her young eyes was so intense that one of the brothers coloured slightly and asked what she was saying. Alex told him: 'She says why don't you buy an aeroplane and take yourselves back to Detroit?'

The brothers had no rejoinder, but their heavy faces registered a genuine amazement. Was there ever such injustice? They called for their bill, announced they were going to the Moolin Rooj, and disappeared shoulder to shoulder into the crowd. Montmartre was healed of its wound, and we got back to our coq-au-vin and burgundy (only a sip for Sonja), with the warm fragrance flooding in and the murmur of voices from the square.

We spent a long time over the meal and afterwards took a taxi to the hotel near the Madeleine. I had fixed the suite for them. It was close-carpeted and very snazzy. There was a canopy over the double bed, and a sea-green bathroom, and a large comfortable lounge with heavy curtains over the long windows.

I only stayed long enough to point out the drinks cabinet. Sonja plumped herself into a deep chair and kicked her shoes off. Alex was standing by the mantelpiece, smiling as he stroked the red hair back from his forehead. I liked them for being so unselfconscious, so pleased with each other. There was no nonsense about 'Won't you stay?' and I left them to their political discussion. Not reality, just an hour or two of peace and safety in an impossible world, but they deserved whatever they could achieve.

The next day was Sunday and I drove Alex down the long straight road beside the Seine to Fontainebleau. The forest was all brown and gold and tranquil under the clear sky, and the ornate grey palace rose up from the past with dazzling splendour. 'Son Palais Prestigieux, Ses Jardins Merveilleux', said the pamphlet. What an understatement! Alex was an exhausting sightseer, and after the palace we had to tour the nearby American Army quarters, where he was amazed almost to tears by the clean and solid buildings, the garage to every house. The Red Army, he said, lived mostly in wooden huts. Oh, my people, my poor people!

On the way back he talked about Sonja. He seemed depressed. 'Yes, she's a lovely girl, she's fine, we're happy together. But what's the use of it all? I can't be my real self with her because she knows nothing about my work. She's like all the others. There's nothing permanent, not ever, not anywhere. Why does everything have to be so difficult?'

But on Monday, when his first week of factory visits and business appointments began, he was his old cheerful self. Everything went well that week. Each night we took him to the house in the crescent, and before leaving he was given the rendezvous for the following evening. The Intelligence men were delighted, but as the days passed I could see the strain growing in him. Paris was heaven, and he didn't want to leave, he wanted to stay for ever. At the end of the week my people told me that I was to go away for a few days because it was important for Alex and me not to be too closely associated. If I went away now, while Alex was in Paris, the Russians would conclude that there was no special link between us. I had previously been asked by my companies to go to Yugoslavia for the Zagreb Trade Fair. I would not have gone if I had been wanted in Paris, but now my people advised me to go, to maintain my image as a genuine businessman. All the time I was away I wondered how Alex was getting on, I pictured him in Paris with the precious days passing.

When I got back he had only a week left. He did not speak of his departure but I could feel it hanging over him. I asked him how things had been going and he said very well, there had been no trouble. Had he seen Sonja? Only once or twice. And the other girls, what about them? Yes, he had met two of them, they were all right, they had given him a good time. 'Anyhow, you're back now,' he said, 'that's the great thing.'

But not for long, that was what worried him. He had got used to working with me, and now the long winter in Moscow lay ahead and no one could think of a good and legitimate reason why I should go there once more. Already in Moscow he had been introduced socially to the British wife who lived there, who was to work with him in my absence. Now she was in Paris, on leave with her husband, and Alex and I met her in the hotel suite. We went through the signals and operating procedures and Alex was very polite and professional, but I knew what he was thinking. When you have worked with someone for a long time, especially in danger, you get superstitious. You do not like the idea of a change.

On the second evening there occurred an incident which, ludicrous though it was and harmless though it turned out, showed what a strain Alex was under. He did something which I had never known him do before. He broke an important rule.

All day he was at a factory, and in the early evening, by way of a change in routine, he snatched a couple of hours with the Intelligence people, after which he was going to meet me at nine o'clock for dinner. Again for variety we arranged to rendezvous at the bar of a restaurant in the Avenue Friedland. It had been a glorious day, but at sunset the wind changed, bringing rain. It was bucketing when I crossed the avenue and reached the restaurant.

Alex was not there and the restaurant, being on the Monday routine, was closed. We had overlooked this.

For any rendezvous you must never hang about. If your contact is not there on time, you go away for a minute or two and come back.

I walked down to a kiosk, bought a paper, and returned. Still no Alex. Up the street to a shop window and back. Down the side street and back. Round the block and back. The rain bounced off the pavement, the gutters were full of swirling water, there was a gusty wind, people were hurrying with umbrellas, shouting at taxis, and as the minutes passed I found it hard to keep contact with the doorway without being too obvious. Probably no one else noticed me, but I noticed myself. A quarter past nine. What could have happened? It was most unlikely that Intelligence had kept him when they knew he had an appointment. I walked slowly up and down the opposite pavement, keeping the doorway in view. At half past nine I was fighting back ridiculous and sinister thoughts. It was twenty to ten when I came up to the side street, turned the corner, and found Alex in a doorway near the restaurant.

He was not alone.

He was cuddling two girls in shiny raincoats, one red, one black, an arm round each, and he greeted me with a whoop of joy:

'Hey, Greville, look here! Look what I've got. Aren't they gorgeous?'

'Wonderful,' I said. 'Come on, Alex, that's enough. Let's go.'

'One for you and one for me. You can choose first. How about that?'

The girls smiled at me professionally, and I said:

'Where did you find these two?'

'Never mind, I found them.'

'Well, send them back.'

'Greville, we can't do that. We can't just tell them to go away. Not fair.'

I took out my wallet. I had a fund for such emergencies. My French was limited. I could have said '*Combien?*' but I felt a little more explanation was necessary.

'We'll have to pay them off,' I said. 'We can be nice about it.'

'But Greville . . .'

'You know the rules,' I said.

My French was bad, but Alex's was non-existent. It was up to me. I doubt if the cocottes understood me, but they understood the francs. With shrill cries they accepted two hefty wads into their handbags. But they still clung to Alex's arms.

'What's the matter now?' I said.

'What's the matter?' repeated Alex profoundly. 'Everything's fine.'

'Vamoose,' I said to the girls. 'Go away.'

They answered quickly, much too fast for me, but in the end I got the message. 'My God,' I said. 'We're in trouble!'

'Why, Greville? What is it?'

'It's no use, Alex. They won't go. They say they have received their present and they insist on finishing their job!'

To the true professional, I suppose, to be paid for nothing is almost as bad as to work for nothing. But it was no time for the ethics of labour. I grabbed the girls, pulled them away from Alex, and summoning almost my entire French vocabu-

lary—'*Excusez-moi, mesdemoiselles! Vous êtes très gen-
tilles! Merci bien! Au revoir!*'—I pushed them gently but
firmly into the rain. They stalked away like two parakeets,
one red, one black, and I hustled Alex to the nearest restaurant I could find. I offered to make a telephone call, but
Alex said grandly that if he couldn't have the girls he wanted
he would have none, and even afterwards at the Moulin
Rouge his applause was decidedly frosty.

The weather, having turned, remained bad. The sun had
lost its warmth, at least half of each day was dismal with rain,
and one morning I saw fog through the bedroom window. It
cleared by lunchtime, but it signalled the presence of autumn
and the coming of winter.

Alex still performed his dual duties with skill and deter-
mination. The Soviets were pleased with the material and
information he obtained at the factories and the contacts he
made in industry, and Allied Intelligence were more than
pleased with his performances at the house in the crescent.
But to me there was a change in Alex. The old lighthearted-
ness had gone. He did his work now with grim efficiency. The
lack of sleep alone would have beaten most men, but with
Alex it was not the physical demands that mattered, it was
the thought of leaving Paris and returning to the winter in
Moscow. One night at the Lido, probably the best drilled
spectacular in the world, he brightened up a little. 'This is
good, Greville. It's not just the girls, it's so well done, so
perfect, it's an art, less serious than the ballet.' But there was
still the shadow.

On the last day he had no duties except to put in an appearance at the Embassy cocktail party. In the morning we
went back to the Louvre. It was a grey chilly morning and
the huge silent galleries were almost empty. We were not
experts in painting. Where our fancy was struck, we stopped,
and where it was not, we moved on, but I felt that the masters
were making their point without any art patter from us. We

looked mostly at the Italians, and Alex stood for minutes in front of the lush massive canvases, in silence, as if he wanted to draw out and retain the beauty for himself. Titian's Madonna with the Rabbit, Giorgione's Concert, La Belle Jardinière of Raphael, and the Rubens pictures of Marie de Medici, the lifelike limbs and the rich feasts of colour, but more than this, the achievement. 'They're finished, Greville, they're perfect, they're there for ever.' But in all the Louvre, the painting which impressed him most was a Leonardo, not the Mona Lisa, at whom he shook his head, but John the Baptist. He stood for a long time, staring at the strange face, the shaft of light in the dark passage, and at last said quietly, 'He could be one of us.'

We lunched at a small Basque restaurant and decided that in the evening, after he had finished at the Embassy, we would get Sonja and one of the English girls and have a last party of our own. He said would I get Toni, the red-head, she was the best of the bunch he had met while I was is Zagreb, 'And there's one thing,' he said, 'that I'd better warn you about. When I met Toni before, I told her I was from Belgrade, of course, and she wanted to know all about me, so just for a gag I said I was a famous actor.'

'Well, that's almost true, isn't it?'

'Maybe,' he smiled. 'Anyhow, I said I was here to discuss a big film, so when we meet this evening we'll have to carry on with the story. You'd better be a film man too—or does she know you?'

'I've only set eyes on her once in London. She doesn't know who I am.'

'You can be the director,' said Alex. 'I'll explain to Sonja, she'll love it.'

It was not important, but it was typical of Alex, his need to escape, to mix things up, to reach out for other worlds than his own.

After lunch I telephoned Toni and fixed the suite in the

hotel, and after that we went shopping in the Galeries Lafayette. I took him there because we had a girl specially installed in case he wanted a guide round one of the big stores. She was a French girl, a pretty little blonde with a snub nose and saucy eyes. Her name was Jeanne. She was not an agent, but she had been vetted and was under our control. I did not tell Alex this, because he was a little touchy about being supervised, though he knew the importance of it as well as anyone, how a single careless word to the wrong person (and all unknown people were potentially wrong) could undo the work of years.

He said he wanted to buy presents for his family, and if moralists object to the idea of a party in Paris one night and a family reunion in Moscow on the next, I can only say that Alex acted as he had to act, that his wife and daughter were still a warm and true part of his life, and that when he was allowed to be with them, he treated them, as far as I could judge, with a more genuine affection than many husbands, including some of the moralists.

I wanted him to enjoy every possible moment of this last day, so I handed him over to Jeanne and moved off to do some shopping of my own. I saw them heading towards the parfumerie, and when we met again Alex had his arms full of parcels and a look of conquest in his eyes.

'Jeanne is coming to the party,' he announced. 'She's going to meet us at the Villa d'Éste.'

When we got outside I said it was bad having two men and three girls, and Alex said airily:

'Well, get another man, anyone you like. And don't forget to tell him about the film set-up. He can be the producer.'

We parted to our hotels and I said I would pick him up at nine o'clock. I had a bath and a change and then set about finding the third man. We could not take just anyone to the private suite, it had to be one of our own men, and the first two I thought of, because of their liveliness, had other engagements. Another, who would have done splendidly, had flown back to England, and several more said they didn't like blind dates. In the end I persuaded 'Blackie' (not his real name) to come along. I told him it would be a nice quiet evening, because Blackie was a very quiet man. He had a fantastic war record organising an escape route in the Balkans, and he was now a first-class agent, but whatever his weaknesses were, they were certainly not wine or women.

I told him to be at the Villa d'Éste at nine-thirty, so that the rest of us could be already at the table and there would be no chance of his backing out.

At nine o'clock I picked up Alex and Sonja, went to the restaurant where Jeanne and Toni were waiting, and found our table. At nine-twenty-nine I went out to the foyer and found Blackie looking at his watch. I explained quickly about his being a film producer. Blackie looked alarmed. 'Wait a minute, Greville, what is all this? What am I supposed to say?'

'Just talk big,' I said, piloting him towards the table. 'You're the film boss. You've got all the money, you control everything.'

A more reluctant producer never sat down to a party, but Blackie in spite of his inexperience was a good scout at heart, and after the second round of champagne cocktails he began to get the hang of it so well, and shot such a grand line about his plans for a film on the French Revolution that Toni and Jeanne, listening agog to the sums of money he was mentioning, started to pay more attention to Blackie than to Alex himself. The girls were a fine trio, the red-head, the blonde and the jet black. Toni, of course, was a professional party girl, smart and smiling, ready to laugh at almost anything. Jeanne looked as if she had stepped straight out of a tired businessman's calendar, and Sonja, the demure, had evidently learnt a lot during her stay in Paris. We had a wonderful dinner based round Pheasant à la Souvaroff, and afterwards we danced and watched the floor show, and all the time I could see Alex getting more excited and restless, wanting it to be more of a party than any party could ever be, not liking the noise to stop for a moment, always ready with a toast or a story, getting more and more ambitious with his film anecdotes, and how pleased he was to be breaking away from his 'native' country. Fortunately Toni and Jeanne were as vague as the rest of us about the Yugoslavian film industry.

By one o'clock we had all had enough dancing and went back to the suite in the hotel. Alex carried a large carton of bottles, and another which he refused to open. We went into the suite and Alex took the champagne out of the carton, and from the other produced chocolates and perfume for the girls, and an enormous bottle of Je Reviens. Blackie asked if the Je Reviens were for him, and Alex laughed and said no for everyone, and before anyone could stop him he took out the stopper and started shaking the perfume all over the carpet, till the room smelt like a harem.

We put on the radio and turned down the lights and drank and danced a little, smooching around, and Blackie drank a glass of champagne standing on his head, and Alex and Sonja gave us a full-blooded Cossack dance, and everyone said what the hell of a time we were having. But somehow it wasn't quite the party it should have been, not what Alex was imagining. It was no one's fault. The girls were as warm and friendly as could be, and Blackie showed the very best of his hidden depths, but the fact was that by four o'clock we were all dead tired and ready for bed.

And to bed we went, saying fond good nights in the cold street, and climbing into our various taxis.

The next morning I took Alex to the airport. The flight was from Orly this time, and halfway there the fog suddenly closed in and we feared we would be late, but when we arrived the airport was fogbound, and we had to wait four hours. The waiting was terrible, an unexpected refinement of doubt. Was the fog a sign for Alex? Did the gods caution him to stay? The place was half empty, and we walked around and drank coffee and brandy and talked about the good times we had had in Paris and how it would not be long till the next meeting and so on. But we were kidding ourselves, we knew that we could not tell when or how we would see each other, and that if Alex went back now, there was the winter ahead.

When at last the departure was announced we walked to the Customs, and at the door Alex stopped, and for a moment I thought he was going to turn round and come back to Paris and safety. He dropped his cases and stood there without speaking, and I waited and hoped.

Suddenly he seized my hand, then picked up the cases, and said, 'No, Greville, I have work to do,' and was gone.

I watched the take-off through the window. There was still some fog about, and the sky was opaque and heavy, and the plane was hardly airborne before it disappeared.

# 4

# Vladimir

## I

'Now you are going to be punished for your crimes. Now you will learn to respect us.'

This was the last thing the General said to me in Lubyanka. As I leave Moscow, sitting between two plain-clothes men in the back of the curtained car, looking past the driver and the deputy warden at the flat grey drizzling landscape, I think of what the General said. I admit the first part but deny the second. Punishment, yes. Respect, never. The car ride takes over three hours and I do not let my thoughts linger too much on the past or the future because both are bad. Lubyanka was bad and Vladimir will, I am sure, be worse. I do not want a pain in the head from thinking of such things, so I observe what I can through the windscreen.

The land is flat and barren and the horizon is lost in rain. The road is terrible. There are no forests, no mountains, no factories, no petrol stations, no inns, no modern buildings, no organised farming, nothing but broken hedges enclosing fields of meagre crops, and here and there small clusters of wooden huts, and every ten or fifteen miles a village. The church with its round dome is decayed and the wooden houses are unpainted and there is a single water tap for the village. Sometimes out of the rain a lorry with crates wobbles towards us and vanishes behind. Once we stop and I am pushed out by the roadside. Hurry up, dog, get it over with. The road is almost straight, and at the end will be Vladimir.

I know about Vladimir. It is an ancient city but the prison is only sixty years old. The Czar built it for political prisoners, and after the revolution it became a stopping place for Soviet prisoners who were walking from Moscow to the salt mines of Siberia. It is a hundred and fifty miles from Moscow to Vladimir, and the lucky prisoners died on the road to Vladimir, and the less lucky died on the road after Vladimir, and the really unlucky prisoners reached the salt mines. Vladimir is a special prison, specially bad. It holds two thousand prisoners and none have escaped. Most of the Soviet prisoners die there. They are given a term, then another and another till they die. Many German and Japanese generals have known Vladimir. Now I am going to know it. I drive towards Vladimir across the flat drenched muddy immeasurable acres of the Soviet Union.

It is twilight and raining when we reach the city and stop outside the cracked gloomy walls of the prison. The city appears almost lifeless. Many houses gape idiotically down at us with open doorless mouths and broken skulls. A few ragged citizens amble at street corners. I have a wild wish that it will take us a long time to reach the prison, but we are here in no time at all. Opposite the prison is the cemetery. A brass band is playing a funeral dirge for dead comrades. The lash of cold rain hurts my cheeks.

In the damp stone entrance lobby the deputy warden from Lubyanka hands me over to the prison major and goes. He does not say goodbye to me.

The prison major does not speak to me. He gives an order and my suitcases are thrown on the floor. Round the walls lounge fourteen Soviet soldiers. I call them soldiers because they wear uniforms. Their caps are flat-a-back, their shoes are grubby, and their ankle-length greatcoats are frayed and spotted. They have kitbags, so I suppose they are on draft.

Thin wet cigarettes hang from their mouths. When I come in, the soldiers start jeering with rude gestures.

There are two female guards dressed as soldiers. The females open my cases and tip my belongings on to the floor. The Major kicks some of the bottles across the floor, but he does not speak to me. He intends me to become degraded, to become an animal—and why should he speak to an animal?

When my belongings have been rammed back into the cases, a drab civilian-girl interpreter screams, 'Strip off!' When I am naked, the females stare at my crutch and point and laugh. My mouth and ears and armpits are searched for contraband. Then my head is pushed down to my knees, and my behind feels the hard thrusting jab of metal, up and up. I have nothing concealed up there and only blood comes out. I can feel it on my legs. I cry: 'Soviet culture!' and the females roar with laughter. They are laughing not at what they hear but at what they see. It is a most hilarious sight for them. When the interpreter girl translates my 'Soviet culture' the Major makes no comment except to stare at me.

I am taken to a tiny cell and left naked for two hours. There is a deathly chill. I clap my hands and slap my body. Maybe I will end by dying of cold, but not on the first evening!

Now I am given my underclothes and shoes without laces. My suitcases are brought and I am told to pick them up. I carry the cases back to the entrance lobby and dump them on the floor. My leg is hurting. I announce I cannot carry the cases. 'Carry them!' screams the interpreter.

I answer, 'I can't.'

'Carry them!'

'I can't.'

After some more yelling a guard picks up the cases and I am marched across the prison compound to the hospital wing. For isolation, not because I am reckoned in any way unfit. I am received by the captain in charge of the block, and after some hanging about am taken to a cell on the first floor.

When the guard brings in my cases, I register in some corner of my shaking mind a tiny victory.

The cell is similar to Lubyanka, but several grades filthier. Instead of eau-de-Nil, the lower walls are chocolate brown. The whitewashed ceiling is crumbling. The radiator is a single fluted pipe protected by bars. The iron bed is rusty and the table unscrubbed for years, but the worst thing in the cell is a dented ex-oil-drum with a badly fitting lid. This, I am told, is my lavatory. Surely someone has slipped up, allowing me a lid.

The door is slammed and I am alone. For a long time I sit on the bed. There is nothing else to do. I cannot begin cleaning till I get some *Pravda*. My joints ache and my stomach pinches. Leaving out self-pity, which is not allowed, I have to admit that this is going to be more difficult than Lubyanka. In the early days at Lubyanka I still had reserves of strength, but now these reserves have gone. I am a camel who has almost finished his hump. However bad the food is, I must make the very most of it. When at last the flap in my cell door is opened and a female guard pushes in my supper I jump up with a foolish eagerness. I am foolish all right. My supper is a bowl of fish soup and a mug half full of tea. There is a kettle of water for topping up the tea and washing the bowl and spoon. The fish soup is bitter and floating with eyes. I swallow the soup, eyes and all. Maybe fish eyes are good for me. Who knows? At least they are easier to swallow than the sheep's eyes once offered to me so ceremoniously by a Moroccan host.

I lie on the bed under the thin coarse blanket but I cannot sleep. The light seems brighter than in Lubyanka. When sleep does come it is suddenly broken by the necessity of leaping up and running to the oil-drum. There is no paper.

At six o'clock I am woken again by the Soviet National Anthem blaring through the loudspeaker over the door. Breakfast comes—porridge as thick as mud and not much tastier, a piece of black bread, and three small lumps of sugar. The sugar is for the day, and I only put one lump in my tea. After breakfast a female guard comes in and points to the oildrum and I pick up the drum and follow her to the main lavatory which is a cubicle with a hole in the concrete floor. I empty the drum down the hole and I see that the edges of the hole are spattered with bloodstained phlegm, and I remember that tuberculosis flourishes in Soviet prisons. In the wash-house beyond there is more cough-blood in the basins and all over the sludge-covered floor. I am given a shower from the rusty ceiling rose. My small tablet of soap is hard and my towel is half the size of a washing-up cloth. I scrub myself furiously because I am thinking of the tuberculosis. The towel is soon sodden, and when I am dressed and back in the cell my body is still damp. I do violent exercises but it is afternoon before my body feels dry. Maybe it is as well that showers come only once in ten days.

My next visit is to the barber, who with clippers shaves off my moustache, my beard, and all the hair off my head. Hello, scalp! I am pleased to make your acquaintance. It is strange to think that you have been hiding for all these years. Allow me to rub you.

I am back in my cell and still rubbing my scalp with friendly attention when the door opens and I am told to roll up my mattress and blanket and bring my spoon and mug. I follow along to a new cell where there are two beds, and on one bed sits a tall frail-looking boy of about twenty-three. When we are alone he introduces himself. His name is Kelly.

His name is not Kelly. I call him Kelly because he is still alive. I do not know where he is, but I know he is safe. One day perhaps Kelly will wish to tell his own story and he must be free to tell it from his own point of view. But I too must speak about Kelly, first because he is a brave boy, and second because our stay together in Vladimir has a special significance in my story.

So here is tall frail Kelly. The first thing I notice is his shyness. He speaks very quietly and looks at the floor. He starts to tell me that he was tried *in camera* and sentenced to eight years. He has served one year, five months in the south and now in Vladimir, but here I change the subject. These things are best discussed in the open air. He is on sick diet, which includes some white bread and a little milk. It is a slim margin between death and life, but, as soon as the first meal is brought in, Kelly cuts his bread in two and pours half his milk into my mug. I protest, but Kelly refuses to touch his food unless I share it with him, so I share it.

He has cigarettes and tobacco which he does not smoke and one book a week from the prison library. He shows me a list. Dickens, Mark Twain, Thackeray, Dostoievsky, Arnold Bennett, Shakespeare, Cronin and a fair selection of old-fashioned detective stories. Rich food for the mind and poor food for the body. Kelly has been starved. They did not wish him to die, so now he is on a sick diet. But he still looks awful.

The second thing I notice about Kelly is his strong belief in God. When bedtime comes he starts looking at me with a reproving, almost hostile, expression. A few nights later he is mumbling to himself, so I say to him that if anything is worrying him he must tell me. We are boxed in together and it will not help to get on each other's nerves. So what is he mumbling about? And Kelly explains that he wishes to say his prayers, but is embarrassed to say them aloud when I am around. 'Go ahead, Kelly. Pretend I am not here. I do not say prayers myself, but that must not stop you.' So Kelly kneels down and says his prayers, and I turn my back and pretend to inspect the rules on the wall. Kelly has been a long time alone and has built up a privacy for himself, and it is important for this privacy to be preserved. There are two basic ways of coping with imprisonment. The inward way, which is Kelly's, of building a world of your own thoughts so intense that it becomes your reality, making your prison life an insignificant dream. And the outward way, which is mine, of filling your days with cleanings and polishings and exercises and schemes for confusing the ridiculous and despicable Soviets. Either way can be effective, it depends which sort of person you are. Kelly and I are different sorts, but our problem is to co-exist, and we solve it by granting one another an absolute freedom of behaviour.

So I notice Kelly's shyness and his sense of God. But the third and most important thing I notice is the emergence of his bravery.

To be brave you must first be afraid, for only a fool has no fear. The question is how you get over it. I see that Kelly is somewhat afraid of the guards, because at six o'clock next morning, when the National Anthem blares through our wall-speaker, he stands up while I sit on the bed. When the guard bursts in and yells and Kelly (who knows Russian) translates that we are required to stand for the National Anthem, I shout back, 'I am not standing up, not till the day I join the Red Army!' Kelly passes this on and the guard rushes at me and hauls me to my feet, and the moment he lets go I sit down. Up, down, up, down. By this time the Anthem is over and the guard yells that my behaviour will be reported and goes out, and for the rest of the day I work on Kelly, explaining the necessity of standing up to them by not standing up.

Next morning I wait to see what Kelly will do. When the Anthem starts, and we can see the eye of the guard through the spy-hole, I watch Kelly clenching his hands as he sits on the bed. It is like watching someone on the high board who has never taken a dive before. But when the guard comes in Kelly goes on sitting. The guard heaves him up, but when the guard comes to me Kelly sits down, and when the guard goes to Kelly I sit down. This time, yells the guard, we shall both be reported 'in the book', whatever this may mean. But nothing happens for the present (though it does later when we meet Chevshenko) and we never stand for the Anthem again.

This may sound a small victory, but it is a beginning.

During our first day Kelly never smiled, but after our bob-bing act on the second morning, when the guard goes out, Kelly smiles. This pleases me, because it is not easy to find things to smile about in Vladimir. For instance, sharing the oil-drum. This is a bestial punishment, a degradation impos-sible to find amusing. All you can do is to turn away and not think about the sounds and smells. Soviet culture!

All this is Kelly's story as much as mine, but the thing which for me has special significance is the comparative luxury of these first few weeks in Vladimir, the prison of punishment. 'Now you will be punished,' said the General in Lubyanka. On the long car journey I felt sick with anticipa-tion. My welcome on that first damp night was what I ex-pected. And now here I am, still in my civilian clothes, shar-ing a cell with Kelly who speaks English, sharing Kelly's milk and white bread and his library books and, besides this, allowed a trifle or two from my luggage, a packet of Roth-mans cigarettes, some Nescafé and a pot of Marmite brought by Sheila, and even, now and then, a small piece of meat in the soup. We are free to talk all day, and we exercise together in the row of pens outside the hospital block. There are no interrogations.

It is not a healthy life. We shall not grow fat. But it is assuredly not the worst punishment that Vladimir, death-house of so many thousands, can provide.

The answer is simple. They hope that Kelly and I will say things we shouldn't, will make some comment or revela-tion which may later on be useful for interrogation, and since the guard cannot hear us through the door, and if he could hear would not understand, it is certain that the cell is bugged. So where is the microphone? Well, speaking as an electrician, I would say the microphone is almost certainly inside the loudspeaker on the wall. And lo and behold, the silly Soviets have fitted a plug and socket behind the speaker, so that I can kill the microphone by removing the plug. When Kelly and I wish to speak privately we make a sign, and the plug is withdrawn and replaced afterwards. At least once a week the speaker is taken away and brought back, but the electricians of Vladimir can find nothing wrong with the microphone because it works perfectly. Somewhere in Vladimir hundreds of feet of tapes are storing up our enthralling conversations about Arnold Bennett, and meals we have eaten, and nights out we have enjoyed. Kelly is fed because they do not wish him to die, and I am allowed to share because they cannot prevent it. The deputy warden, a mean bastard if ever I saw one, does not approve of this. I can see him eyeing me with a wait-till-I-get-you-alone expression, and I have no doubt it will be a sorry day for me when Kelly and I are parted.

In the meantime, after our success over the National Anthem, we set to work on a new mischief, the great tobacco racket.

Nearly all prisoners want tobacco, but especially those who are in the hospital block for sickness rather than segregation. If you are sick your tobacco ration is withheld as an incentive to quick recovery, so Kelly and I decide to spread a little happiness by passing round the tobacco he does not want.

First we need a waterproof container, and here we are lucky, because among the things I was able to extract from my luggage is a plastic bag (the old receptacle of dirty socks on my travels) and some sellotape. We need something waterproof because the hiding place we have chosen is the water cistern which hangs above the hole in the lavatory floor. The lid of the cistern can be removed, and the bag, full of tobacco, is pushed down under the valve, whence it can be retrieved by the next man in the cubicle. When you leave a cubicle it is searched by a guard, but the guards are looking chiefly for messages written on the wall and do not think of opening the cistern.

But how to let our idea be known?

The answer, we find, is one of the wash-house attendants, himself a prisoner of ten years. So the news is spread, and the illegal tobacco racket is established and the bag comes back over the wall of our exercise pen, and many times we hear cracked voices coming from unidentifiable windows calling an attempt at my name . . . 'Binny's all right! Kelly's okay!' And one morning a face more daring than it should be (for to be caught speaking to me would certainly bring a beating) lingers long enough to catch my eye, and calls out, 'Never mind, Binny, the Chinese liberate you!' The man who risks a beating to call this has probably been in his cell for years. He will rot there and die there. His courage encourages me.

To face Chevshenko, for instance.

Chevshenko is a colonel in the Red Army and a high officer in the K.G.B., the Civilian Security Service. His parish is an enormous area east of Moscow, and his headquarters is in Vladimir. Chevshenko is a colonel, but he dresses as a civilian and has civilian attitudes, and this is really the great difference for me between Vladimir and Lubyanka. It is true, I believe, the world over that servicemen will never behave quite as badly as civilians. Army criminals are children compared with the criminals of civvy street, and it is the same among those who have charge of the criminals. In Lubyanka even at my worst moments I always felt somewhere a tingle of military discipline, but in Vladimir there is none. True, the wardens and guards are dressed in uniform, but the attitude stems from Colonel Chevshenko, and Chevshenko is a toad, cold and poisonous, whose venom is entirely without discipline and therefore without limit.

I meet Chevshenko during my fourth week in Vladimir. I am taken to his filthy office for interrogation, and Kelly is brought along because he knows Russian.

Chevshenko is sprawling at his desk. He is sloppily dressed

and fat. His left forearm is resting on the desk, and I notice
his watch which is twice the thickness of an ordinary watch.
This, I know, means that the watch contains a microphone.
The transmitter will be hidden under his jacket, and the leads
to the microphone will be strapped to the underside of his
arm. That is why he keeps his arm so rigid on the desk, and
also why every fifteen minutes precisely, even in the middle of
a sentence, he jumps up and goes out to ensure the tapes are
changed on the recorder in the next room.

For two minutes he says nothing, casting toad glances at
me as I lounge against the wall with my hands in my pockets.
Suddenly he shouts hoarsely, and Kelly translates that we
have got to stand to attention. Kelly himself is already to
attention, and when I keep my hands in my pockets, the toad
leaps up and swipes me backhanded across the face.

'So what,' I shout.

'Attention,' says Kelly.

'Tell him to drop dead. I'm not in his blasted army. Nor
are you, Kelly. You did all right for the National Anthem.
Put your feet apart, Kelly. Hands on hips. That's better.'

When Toad hears this he yells for the guards, and two apes
come in and haul us into some form of attention, but it is not
a success. Then Toad starts a long harangue, chiefly directed
at me, about this being Vladimir, the punishment prison, and
the trial being over and nothing to look forward to but years
of whatever he chooses to do with me, and how I will find
Vladimir a different place from Lubyanka—all of which I
know already. I am not feeling at my best this morning. My
stomach is a horrid jumble of black bread and fear, but as
Chevshenko continues with his spiel about knowing everything and how the K.G.B. has methods of getting anything
out of anybody, I can only answer that he is wasting his time
and that I have nothing to add to what I admitted during the
trial. Each fifteen minutes on the dot Chevshenko goes out
to change the tapes, and at the end of the third tape he holds

a cigarette in his yellow-stained fingers and addresses me
The words sound nasty in Russian, and when they are repeated in Kelly's soft translation they have an added nasti-
ness:

'Very well, we shall see. Up to now you have been too
well treated, but you are going to learn. I say, you are going
to learn. It is reported that you refuse to stand up for the
National Anthem of the Soviet Union. We shall not waste
time by lifting you to your feet every morning. We have other
methods of persuasion in Vladimir. You are going to wish you
had never come to Vladimir.'

I wish this already, but I say nothing, and we are marched
back to our cell, and for three weeks there is a lull with no
more interrogations. Perhaps Chevshenko has not yet given
his instructions, for the food and the books continue, and we
find a guard who in return for a plastic box (another of my
luggage treasures) gives us sugar cubes and Russian
cigarettes and on two occasions a large sandwich filled with
smelly but welcome salami. And then one morning the deputy
warden comes in and gives me his meanest look and tells
Kelly to pack his traps because he is leaving.

When we are alone Kelly starts speculating about his
transfer. For a Soviet prisoner change is never welcome. The
Soviets will never improve your condition and the thought of
somewhere worse than Vladimir is truly depressing. As it
turned out Kelly was taken to the notorious 'Number Five'
at Mordova in the fever-ridden swamps of the south, where
he survived and was released some months later. But we do
not know this at the moment, and I find it hard to cheer Kelly
up, and we finish by shaking hands and making the thumbs-
up sign to one another with all the enthusiasm we can muster,
which is very little. When the door slams and I hear Kelly's
footsteps dying away in the corridor, I sit down feeling very
lonely and slightly sick.

Berlin, Checkpoint Heerstrasse. Time: Dawn. Date: April 22, 1964.
After eleven months in prison, Wynne is exchanged for the Russian spy,
Gordon Lonsdale. The group on the left is Russian; the group on the
right is British and is about to enter the car to return to the West with
Wynne.

The author before his arrest.

The author after imprisonment.

The author—photographed after his release, in the prison uniform
which he brought back from Russia.

Forty-eight hours I am left alone, and then my comfort abruptly ends. My civilian clothes are taken away and I am left naked for several hours before the prison uniform is brought and thrown on the floor. The uniform stinks, and with revulsion I draw on the thin scratching trousers. The deputy warden is lounging happily against the door. He tells me, through the girl interpreter, that none of my personal belongings will be allowed in my new cell. Two guards are barging round, stuffing my treasures into a sack, and of course I am determined that something shall be saved, however small, but the guards are thorough and tough, and my only achievement is one handful of Kelly's tobacco which I thrust into my trouser pocket. Then I am marched to the floor above and into my new cell. This is the filthiest of all my cells, and worse than the dirt is the smell. It is a vegetable, mineral and animal smell. First the old thin blanket and the rotting table leg. Then the rust smell from the bed and radiator bars. Then the smell from the last man's oil-drum in the corner. But above and beyond this amalgam, somewhere in the foetid air that my nostrils must however unwillingly intake, there is another unidentifiable odour, strange and sickening. I wander round trying to track down this odour, dreading to find it, and come at last to the mattress, the unmistakable source. The stench, for sure, is animal. I am smelling the last man's body. At this moment, faintly through the closed window, comes the sound of the brass band in the cemetery, and as I recoil from the mattress I have a fancy, unprovable yet overwhelming, that I am inhaling the last dank impregnation from the corpse they have chucked into the muddy hole outside. I am so nauseated by this image that I hardly care when I notice that the oil-drum in the corner has no lid.

I open the top flap of my window. The summer air, Soviet though it may be, at least dilutes the smell. The window is of opaque wired glass, and I see a tiny hole which I enlarge with my spoon. So now I can see the compound below and, with this encouraging vista, I set about my old routine of cleaning and polishing with the lumps of sodden *Pravda* from the lavatory.

For several days I am busy, but the work is harder than before. My diet is back to slimy bread and fish-eye soup and my body is slower to generate its energy. Sometimes my hands lose their grip, and the wet lump of *Pravda* drops on the floor, and it is seconds before I can muster myself to pick it up. I am missing my chats with Kelly, especially first thing in the morning when I wake to a silent day and last thing at night when I lie in silence unable to sleep for the steel-pin ache in my hip. In some strange way my thoughts too become slower, and it takes me a whole morning to realise that I am in danger of succumbing to a fatal idleness and despair.

So how about a little mischief? But the method I select— and here comes the incident of the fishing lines and the tobacco—has a terrible outcome.

The hospital block is a long five-storeyed building with eighteen cell windows in each storey. The top row of windows is the hospital theatre and administration section, the second floor is the wards for those prisoners who are under actual medical treatment. The third and fourth rows are for male political prisoners who require segregation. The bottom row is for female prisoners.

In the centre of the building at the rear is an arched doorway, and a few feet from the doorway is the line of exercise pens similar to those on the roof of Lubyanka, high walls topped with barbed wire and open to the sky. On the far side of the pens is a raised platform where two armed guards continually patrol, to prevent communication between prisoners and especially the exchange of tobacco.

It may sound unlikely that in front of two guards, who have a full view of everything, tobacco could be transferred from

the pens to the cells. Yet it was accomplished, and I see it
accomplished not once but many times.

Exercising in the pen I can see, above the open window
flaps, the heads of prisoners, the shaved skulls and the thin
staring faces whose age it is impossible to guess. They are
hoping to make contact, which is forbidden, and most of all
they are hoping for tobacco. Their method of obtaining it is
remarkable.

Prison socks have a reinforced toe-cap, and this toe-cap
is cut off to make a small bag. The rest of the sock is un-
ravelled into a fishing line, and the bag is attached to the line
and weighted with a pellet of soap. If contact is made with a
prisoner in one of the pens, a sock-bag comes flying down
and is filled and drawn up again, while the guard's eyes are
in another direction. Many times I have seen the flying lines
and I have never seen a line observed by a guard. It sounds
hardly credible but it is true. The prisoners have had years of
practice.

So one morning I decide to help. I plan to send up not a
single cigarette but a whole bagful of tobacco. It will be a
last present from Kelly, though if Kelly had been with me I
might not be making my dreadful mistake.

The face appears, sure enough, and the moment I nod to it
down flies the line and the bag lands within two feet of me,
and I quickly stuff it full of tobacco, and the bag is hoisted
up towards the window. But I have been too generous, for the
line breaks under the weight. The bag falls to the ground, and
the line is left festooned from the window bars.

With horror I wait for the guards to notice, but the line is
thin and nothing happens, and soon I am taken back to my
cell. For five minutes I pretend to hope, then in charges the
deputy warden with his interpreter girl, and I am questioned
about the sock-bag outside my pen. I deny all knowledge of
the bag, and the deputy warden, perhaps because there have
been other prisoners in the pen and he cannot be sure of pin-

ning the guilt, leaves me alone. So I have escaped, but with sickness I think of the tell-tale line hanging from that other window close to mine . . . and now, sure enough, a whistle is blown in the compound, and through the hole in my window I see six big guards come racing from their quarters. They carry black leather belts. I hear their feet pounding up the staircase, and then the beating and the screaming. For ten minutes the crack of leather and the anguished shuddering screams.

Next morning in the exercise pen I dare not raise my eyes to the window but at last I look up, and there above the window flap is hardly a face but the bruised and bloated travesty of a face. A finger is laid against the swollen lips, and the awful head shakes with a reproach I shall never forget. Nor shall I forget that he did not tell them who had filled the tobacco bag.

No margarine now, no scraps of meat in the soup, no pillow for my bed, no cartons of Western cigarettes, no books. Even my dictionary is taken away and with it my calender of crosses. It is now a fortnight since Kelly left, and nine weeks since I came to Vladimir. Each morning I add one day and repeat the number several times to make sure I shall remember it next morning. One day is like another, and there are no weekends. I am not part of the world, but all the more reason for keeping contact with the world's passage of time. It is summer now and in English high streets girls will be buying swimsuits for their holidays. Here in the vast eastern plain the summer is hot and there is a peculiar feeling of immenseness. The prison faces outwards from the town, and through my window-hole I can see the guards' quarters and the prison walls and nothing else but the asphalt vault of the sky. I suppose it is no bigger than elsewhere but it looks bigger, like the sky at sea. I feel utterly withdrawn and excluded from the world. The distance back to life seems to

grow, and I seem to dwindle and I am afraid of myself, and
the days without books, without even a pencil, without interrogations to break the time, seem very long. So I keep rigidly
to my mental calendar, and it is in the middle of August,
when my friends will be off to France, Italy and the Costa
del Sol, that I am suddenly faced with the challenge of the
oil-drum.

Till now I have been emptying the drum each morning,
but one day the guard does not fetch me, and when I complain the deputy warden appears and informs me with relish
that the privilege has been withdrawn. I ask why, and the
deputy warden smiles and goes out.

The smell is horrible, and it is no help that it is my own.
The oil-drum slowly fills with the stenching product of Soviet
fish. After a week the drum is about to overflow, and in blind
rage I upset the drum, and the brown turdous mess spills over
the floor and oozes under the door. The only response from
outside is a line of cloths stuffed under the crack. I yell and
bang on the door, and when the guard opens it I scream,
'Soviet culture!' The Sergeant is fetched, and I repeat my
comment. The Captain comes, then the Major, then the
deputy warden, then the warden. To each in turn I yell the
two words, but no one understands. I am standing inside the
cell and the growing crowd is standing in the corridor holding its noses, and between us is the mud-filled lake of Soviet
culture. Now an order is given and, after five minutes scowling silence, Chevshenko himself arrives with two armed
guards and the girl interpreter.

Holding your nose for someone else's smell is undignified,
and Chevshenko glares at the crowd, and one by one they take
away their hands. I continue to hold my nose with satisfaction at the agony on their faces.

'You have something you wish to say?' asks the girl, and
I shout with my nose still held tight: 'Tell dem dat such
filth would nebber be seen in de West. Eben our animals

would not tolerate dis. Such stinking foulness is a disgrace to
civilisation.' I gabble this so quickly that the girl shakes her
head helplessly, and I point to the mess and say: 'Nebber
mind, just say "Soviet culture!" Go on, say it!'

The girl hesitates and looks at Chevshenko. He waits,
then barks at the girl, and quietly she utters the two words in
Russian. There is a long silence. I look at Chevshenko but
no one else looks. I wait to be seized and beaten. I do not care.
But I am not seized. Chevshenko turns on his heel, snaps an
order over his shoulder, and walks away. I am taken out for
exercise and, when I come back, I have a new cell, still tatty
and flaking but without the smells. On the bed is a pillow and
in the corner stands a new oil-drum. And the oil-drum has a
lid!

Another victory? But now there is hollowness. Have your
lid, you poor hog. We can starve you till you cease to exist,
alive though you may be.

Next morning Chevskenko sends for me. The girl interpreter is clearly terrified of Chevshenko and hopes I will say
nothing to enrage him. He does not interrogate. He simply
says (I condense):

'You have been given a new cell, but do not imagine this
means we intend to make you comfortable. We shall do whatever is necessary to bring you to your senses. You do not
know what is going to happen next. You will never know. You
are completely in our power. You are growing weaker, I see,
so let us hope you will co-operate before your condition
grows serious. Now . . . you will be given pencil and paper,
and you are to make a full confession of all your activities in
the countries of Eastern Europe. We know it all, of course,
but we wish you to write it down so that we may be sure you
have learnt to respect the Soviet Union. Have you anything
to say?'

'What use would it be? You do not believe what I say.'

'Have you any request?'

'I would like my dictionary.'

'The dictionary will be allowed. And understand one thing—that we have time on our side but you have not. Each day you grow weaker. You have little time.'

So I have my dictionary again, and for the next month I keep my calendar and fill the sheets of paper with drawings of houses and lists of words for spelling practice and sometimes just doodling. The doodles, as far as I can interpret myself, are of a purely mosaic nature. I have read of prisoners whose minds during the long emptiness of days become charged with erotic fancies, who even observe on blank prison walls stupendous orgies. This is not my experience. No lips appear in my doodles, nor any tempting torsos on the flaking white-wash of my walls. Sometimes at night, shielding my eyes from the light above the door, I think of girls I have known, but there is no amorous response from my body, and my dreams are never disturbing. Perhaps it is the diet. Fish eyes, it seems, are not an aphrodisiac.

For four weeks I draw and spell and doodle, and then my papers are taken away, but there is no furious reaction as there was in Lubyanka. Instead I am left with nothing but the emptiness of the days. I do not like this. I would rather talk even to Chevshenko than to no one. My crosses creep into September, and there is a chill in the air, and I feel like a night light burning slowly down to nothing. The sun grows watery, the sky overcast, there is a sudden biting wind, and the hand of winter beckons Vladimir with its grim cold fingers. I have no mirror so I cannot see my face, which is perhaps a blessing, but I can see the thin tendons in my thighs and my scraggy hands, once so powerful and now inept and feeble. When I protest to the guard that my blanket needs shaking, and the guard fetches the deputy warden who, after ten minutes' argument, agrees that I may shake my blanket under supervision, I am taken to the exercise pen with two armed guards and a third to hold the other end of the blanket.

We shake one end each, he vigorously and I weakly, and when I get back to the cell, I am exhausted.

So Vladimir creeps towards winter, and I feel all round me the life of death and suffering. I hear screaming in the night. Sometimes the screams are mingled with the crack of leather which means punishment. Sometimes only the screams, which are new prisoners who are drug addicts crying for what they crave, for what they would gladly suffer any punishment, but will never receive. If they scream too much, they will be given fifteen days in a cell with no window, with only electric light, with no furniture but a wooden bench let down from the wall for three hours each night, with food worse than mine. It does not pay to scream.

In the compound are loudspeakers attached to posts. Continually the speakers blare propaganda, instructions to the prisoners on how to behave for the glory of the Soviet Union. Kelly told me that reports of my trial had been broadcast daily so, when I arrived, the prisoners knew who I was and called my name from their windows. At first it helped to hear my name. All prisoners are comrades, and I was glad of the others. But now I am beyond their help. They have their cells and I have mine and we cannot help each other. London told me to be prepared, if I were caught, to serve five years before release. I have now served five months in Vladimir, so Chevshenko has four years and seven months to play with. I dare not contemplate such a length of time. If only something would happen, some change however unpleasant. And my wish is granted, quite unexpectedly, as Chevshenko had forecast.

Early one evening I am escorted to a van at the prison gates. The van, like the lift in Lubyanka, has a metal compartment where I crouch for a twenty-minute bumping journey. When I am pushed out, it is dark and I see a line of guards with tommy guns, searchlights and Alsatians. At the end of the line I see the shadow of a train in a siding. There are twelve guards and five Alsatians, a flattering but exaggerated force.

The cold mud has begun to freeze, and I slip and stagger as I am pushed down the gauntlet of guards and into a small compartment with black-painted windows and a bench where my knees touch the opposite wall. Stale bread and raw fish are thrown on to the floor. The door is locked and I am left alone for a long time, till at last the train begins its clanking journey into the unknown.

How many hours I cannot tell, it seems all night. I eat the fish and bread and try to wedge myself into a corner, but the bench is too narrow for both halves of my bottom and, whenever I doze off, I fall on the jolting floor. I cannot sleep, yet I am only half awake. I wish to urinate. I bang on the door but no one comes, so I urinate on the floor. Who cares? Many times we stop, and I hear shouts and whistles and the rumble of trolley wheels. Then slowly on, in what direction I do not know, but further from Vladimir. Towards Gorky perhaps. There is a place I have heard of in Gorky, but I do not wish to think about it. Who cares? It does not matter. This feels like a goods train, so perhaps I am now classed not as a passenger but as goods. I remember the soap factory of Nazi Germany. Perhaps I shall become a piece of soap for Chevshenko's bottom. Who knows? Who cares? If Chevshenko dips me in his bath and wipes his body with me he will have lost the opportunity of extracting from me the information he so badly wants. He wants it not for the glory of Russia but for his own glory, to show that he can succeed where the G.R.U. have failed. But he will never succeed. To hell with Chevshenko.

At last, in the cold stillness of what I think must be the early hours, the train stops and I am pulled down to find the same avenue of guards and Alsatians as put me aboard. I cannot tell where I am, but a van is waiting, and the van takes me to the gates of somewhere I know very well.

I am back at Lubyanka.

It is the same lift and a similar cell, but it is not the same Lubyanka. I am given my civilian clothes and left alone all morning, then a breakfast of bread and gruel, then up to a new interrogation room where I find the old general, a different colonel, a new interpreter, and several sour civilians who are clearly the K.G.B. So now it is to be a combined interrogation, the military and the civilians together, and this makes a difference. It is a difference I do not welcome, first because my policy of confusion which worked with a single interrogator will not be so easy with so many questioners, and second because I fear the K.G.B. will have a nasty influence on their soldier comrades.

And how right I am.

On a large table is a pile of tins and cartons which I recognise as part of what Sheila had brought at that short meeting so long ago. Spam, chocolate, Nescafé, Bovril, fruit salad, and cigarettes. Also some photographs of Sheila and Andrew at home and a pile of letters. I like what is on the table, but I do not like the looks on the faces of the K.G.B. My stomach yearns for the food and my heart yearns for the photographs and letters, but I feel sure there will be a price on these luxuries, and at once I decide that whatever price it is I will not pay.

The General speaks, and the interpreter begins:

'Well, Mr. Veen, so you are back in Lubyanka. I am sorry to see you have lost a little weight, but that can soon be remedied. Did you have a good journey?'

'It was quite good—for cattle.'

'Now, Mr. Veen—please! You are here to help us, and we are here to help you.' The General points at the table. 'You see all these good things, this tasty food and the photographs of your home. Would you like to have them? Because they are yours.'

'I know they are mine. My wife brought them several

months ago, but so far they have been confiscated.'

'Well, now you can have them. Providing . . .' There is a long pause. The Colonel hands the General a pile of typewritten sheets clipped together, and the General holds the pile towards me—'providing you sign this confession.'

'I have nothing to confess. I have told you many times . . .'

'You have told us many lies. So we have made out this true confession of all your activities as a spy against the Soviet Union. All we need is your signature.'

So they are getting desperate. Till now they have wanted my whole story in handwriting. To be content with a signature, so easily devalued as the result of duress, is a sign that someone higher up is getting impatient.

I say politely: 'I cannot sign what is untrue.'

'You will sign, Mr. Veen.'

'I will not sign.'

'You will *sign!*' yells the General.

There is a silence. Cold eyes stare at me from hard faces. For a weak moment I hesitate. Then I run to the table and with a sweep of my arm send the tins, the photographs and the longed-for letters flying on to the floor.

The General shouts an order. Two guards grab me and pin my arms and the Lieutenant-Colonel swipes me across the face with all his force. Once. Twice. The third time with closed fist. I fall down and there is a piercing pain in my jaw and my mouth is full of blood.

There is no comment. The General waves his hand and the two guards start to lift me by the armpits, but I wriggle round and shoot my feet out and hang there limp and silent. Somehow they hoist me on to the chair, but at once I slip off and sit on the floor, my head bowed in my hands. I am not sorry for myself. I am not afraid. I am filled with a wondrous glow of hatred and contempt. Fire that I thought was dead has kindled in my belly, I can feel the shock waves thrilling up in my body. These apes have made a huge mistake, they have given me a new strength. Now I do not care what happens, I seriously and truthfully do not care. That single maniacal blow has severed for ever the sad connection between my mind and my body. My mind floats like a spectator. With my body they can do what they please. They will never force the truth from me now. Never.

'Would you like a cigarette, Mr. Veen?'

The interpreter is standing over me. I do not answer.

Questions are barked from mouths I cannot see. Am I ready to talk? Shall we begin with Poland? It was there, was it not, that I started to spy? How was I trained? How was I forced to become an agent against the Soviet Union?

I make no reply. I sit on the floor totally immune, secure in my detestation. After half an hour I am hauled to my feet and marched back to the lift and down to my cell.

There is a little tea left from breakfast, and I wash the blood out of my mouth. My jaw aches, but the sharp pain has gone, and gradually, without the faces and voices to kindle me, the hate waves lie down, leaving me with an icy certainty that whatever happens to me physically I am now mentally beyond the General's power.

It is well for me that I am.

That afternoon there is another long interrogation. No cigarettes and no chair. I am kept standing for three hours. My hip throbs and burns, but I do not care. That night I fall straight to sleep, for how long I do not know. Somewhere in the still hours I am woken and taken up to the big room. Now a strong light beams on to my face. The Colonel is only a voice from the blackness behind the light. Now let us deal with the other Socialist countries, with Rumania, with Czechoslovakia, with Hungary, with Poland. Why were you there? Whom did you meet? To whom did the traitor Penkovsky introduce you? Tell us the names. Who was this man? And this? And this? Tell us the names. We know them, but tell us.

'I do not know. There was no one. You are mistaken. That is not so. I have no recollection.'

On and on, day and night, till time is confused and I hardly know whether it is night or day. I have no watch. My cell has only electric light, and in the interrogation room the curtains are drawn and there is only the bright beam on my face. I am either asleep or awake, that is all I know. I have no exercise. The food is down to Vladimir standards. I am not allowed a shower or a shave. Exactly how long I am in Lubyanka I cannot determine, but it is something between two and three weeks, and all this time I am getting more and more detached from myself, knowing only that sometimes the lift goes up and sometimes down, sometimes my voice is saying No to the voices that question me, and sometimes I am silent and alone in my cell.

And now suddenly, as if by magic, I am in the jolting truck again, and now I am back in Vladimir.

My cell is the same but I am different. Something strange is happening to me, a growing quietness, a slowing down, an infinitesimal approach to some inevitable conclusion, though what this is I do not know. For eight weeks I am left alone.

As in my first cell I can only see through the clear glass of my window flap by jumping up and clinging on to the stanchion, so I make a small spy-hole in the lower opaque glass where it joins the frame. If I am to be confined to the cell it is important to be able to see out, it is essential. I can see my prisoner-comrades marching in batches to the work areas. One morning the whole scene has become white, the snow is here, the rolls of barbed wire on top of the walls look like bolsters of cotton wool. At night it snows again, and from now on the snow will fall every two or three days, pathways in the snow will be trodden by thousands of feet, the snow will freeze and be trodden and freeze again. Vlaidimir settles into the great white freezing silence of winter.

I leave my cell only to visit Chevshenko, who repeats hour after hour, day upon day, that my activities in the satellite countries have established me as a trained spy, that he is waiting for my confession, waiting, waiting, and day upon day my answers, in a voice I hardly recognise, are the same. Eight weeks is one thousand three hundred and forty-four hours. If at the beginning I had been told how long it would be, I could not have believed I would last. But I am not told, and at the end I am still guttering towards the moment I am sure is waiting but cannot name.

Now Christmas is over, though the hiatus in Lubyanka prevents me from knowing exactly when, and the cell is very cold. One evening without warning I am taken to the truck once more, and back to Lubyanka. But this visit I need not describe. The Soviets intend to break me, and their methods are the same as before, the same confusion of nights and days, the same questions, the same answers, the same voices in the blackness, the same blinding light. And still, in the truck going back to Vladimir, the same sense of the approaching, the very slowly approaching moment.

Now the food, instead of getting worse, ceases altogether. For three days I have nothing to eat, only a mug of weak tea each morning and a kettle of tepid water for topping up. Chevshenko does not send for me. All day I am alone and all night. I do not know the difference. What I do know, though still I will not give it a name, is the moment I am waiting for. It must be this, there can be no other . . .

I am floating high in the corner of my cell, I am watching myself, the shrunken motionless creature standing by the bed. His bowed head is shaved. His hands are lost in the too long sleeves of the coarse jacket. He has no movement, no thoughts, almost no life . . . and suddenly there is a sense of falling, of total collapse into the moment he has been waiting for, waiting and waiting . . .

I lie still and helpless. I cannot move. There is a drum-
ming in my head like a gentle swarm of bees.

'Breathe in. Breathe deeply.' There is something over my
face, and I can hear the woman's voice. My lungs are full of a
cold sweet draught, I am drifting back from wherever I have
been, and I see myself in an aircraft, and Alex Penkovsky is
standing on the tarmac, waving to me for the last time.

## II

In October 1961 Alex returned from Paris to Moscow.
A fortnight later he passed material to one of our agents on
the Sadovnicheskaya Embankment, the man in the unbuttoned overcoat, whose password, 'I am from your two
friends who send you a big, big, welcome', so enraged the
representatives of the workers of Moscow at the trial.

For the next month the material reaching London and the
reports that came with it showed that Alex was working with
frenzied energy. In the middle of November he took his wife
for a holiday. She was expecting a new baby in February. Although later at the trial Alex was described as a worthless
degenerate, this was hardly the opinion of his masters at the
time, for they sent the Penkovskys on a month's tour of the
Caucasus and the Black Sea, which by Soviet standards was
an extravagance only justifiable as a reward for Alex's work
on the Committee for Scientific Research.

In late December he started to operate with the British
wife in Moscow, and for a couple of weeks all went well. But
in early January a mildly disturbing report reached London.
After passing over some film in a narrow street, Alex noticed
a small car which moved from its parked position, turned
round, and drove away towards the open square. There were
two men in the car. Alex could not be sure whether this was

an observation, but he was relieved the following week when no car appeared. A week later, however, the same car was waiting in the same area, and Alex immediately told London that he proposed, at least for the time being, to stop using the wife as a contact. For the next two months there were no more meetings in the streets of Moscow. Sometimes, but not too often, Alex could accept social invitations by the British and Americans, and then the precious films and packages would change hands. Apart from this, Alex was forced to use the dead-drop boxes. No agent likes the boxes. When you have put the envelope in the box there is always the terrible suspense until you hear it has been collected, and even if you have not been observed you can never be sure that someone has not observed the collector. It was not till the end of March that Alex again met the British wife at a party and was able to hand over some film and receive the latest instructions from British Intelligence.

Always, every day, I thought about Alex, I could feel the strain and tension that must be building up inside him, and London too was worried, and plans were discussed for getting me to the Union again and, if necessary, for bringing Alex to safety in the West. He could not last for ever. He had done more than enough.

The plan decided was to build caravans for mobile exhibition. London gave me a more or less free hand in their design. We heard that there was to be an International Trade Fair in Helsinki in September, and the idea was that I should take the caravans to Helsinki and be ready to slip along to Leningrad for a private exhibition, if I could arrange this with the Soviet authorities, and to bring Alex out in a hidden compartment. The project was put in hand at once, and meantime I could only wait and hope. Leningrad was the westernmost city of importance in the Soviet Union, and it would not be many miles for Alex to reach safety.

March, April, May. Quick months, the spring coming, the

sudden beauty in the London parks, but to me that year the time passed very slowly. Alex was still giving valuable material but not quite so much or so often as before. I kept thinking of the dead-drop boxes and wishing he were not forced to use them. I could feel what drove him to ask more than once that I should go to Moscow; I felt sure he was missing me. Our agents there were first class, but Alex liked to work with me because he knew me so well, we had done so much together. I remembered his cry when I returned to Paris from Zagreb: 'You're back, that's all that matters.' And now I was two thousand miles away and the months were passing and the only way I could vent my impatience was to chase up the building of the caravans. This I did, to the dismay of all concerned.

The first delay was over the chassis. True to British tradition, there were 'none in stock'. The earliest delivery date was quoted as three months, so to save time an extra £350 was paid for a re-delivery from Scandinavia. In spite of this it was six weeks before the London coachbuilders got the chassis, and when they did, there were still endless procrastinations over components and material. I wrote, I telephoned, I went to the factory at all times of day, and I was met with the usual bland and infuriating excuses. They were doing their best. There were union restrictions. There were labour shortages, which I could well believe when three men did one man's job. There was absenteeism. I was not the only customer on their books. Did I think I should receive preferential treatment? The answer was a capital YES, but I could not explain, I could only agitate. If I had had my own way I would have gone to the Continent, where industrial promises can be relied on, but my people said that the caravans must be British built.

In June we heard that Alex was unwell. It was nothing specific or serious, but the very vagueness alarmed me. I suspected exhaustion rather than illness. I wanted to find out.

London agreed that it was time now for the Soviets to know of my proposals for taking the caravans to Leningrad, and for me to take Alex a message of reassurance. If he felt he could not go on, no one would blame him. Everything would be done to get him out.

On the 2nd July I flew to Moscow.

Alex met me at the airport and I saw at once that what I had feared was true. He looked pale and taut and there was a shocking weariness in his eyes. He gave me a big welcome but even that seemed to exhaust him, and in the car he sat silent for some minutes before he began to tell me what he had been through since January, the first hint of being watched, the growing uncertainty through the spring. It was the K.G.B., he thought, who were watching him. They had observed his meetings with the British wife in whom, very likely, they at first imagined his interest to be purely social. It took the K.G.B. a long time to make up their minds that Alex might be acting for the West. He was a senior army officer and worked for the G.R.U. The K.G.B. would never risk making fools of themselves to the G.R.U. There would be no definite move until the K.G.B. had all the evidence they wanted, preferably a red-handed arrest. 'Which they will never get,' he said with a smile. 'Don't worry, I'll be all right now.' But he did not look all right.

In my room at the Ukraine Hotel we exchanged a large quantity of film. Then we turned on the radio and the water taps for extra noise, and Alex took out a letter he had received from London telling him various plans for his escape, should he decide to come. 'They even speak of a submarine,' he said. 'They're good people, they think of everything.'

'That's right. You've only got to say the word.'

'Well, we shall see. It may not be necessary.'

'Don't leave it too long.'

I told him about the caravans and he asked when they would be ready and I said I hoped by September in time for

Helsinki and Leningrad. We had moved nearer to the radio and turned it up full strength, which explains why the tape-recording played to me later in Lubyanka only had our conversation about the submarine and not about the caravans.

'I must go,' he said. 'It looks bad if I hang around here too much. We'll meet at the Gorky Park restaurant.'

We met for dinner, but it was very different from our dinners in Montmartre. Now he was nervous and unsmiling. I asked about Sonja, and he shrugged and said, 'Oh, she got too serious. You know. She's still in Paris. Best place for her. Besides—we have a new baby now, a daughter.'

'Yes, I heard. How is she?'

'Oh, fine, she's a great kid. Except that she yells a lot, keeps us awake all night sometimes.'

'That's bad.'

'Yes, she's worse than British Intelligence!'

This was more like the old Alex, but it did not last. He hurried through the meal and said we must not stay too long or appear to be talking too seriously. Then he raised his glass in front of his lips and said quietly:

'There's something I want to ask you, something I need.'

'What is it?'

'A revolver. I daren't draw one myself, I would have to sign for the ammunition.'

'I'll have to ask London.'

'Well, ask them. Say it's important. Put it as strongly as you can.'

'I'll do that.'

But in fact London would be able to listen for themselves to Alex's request. Under my shirt I had a tape recorder. London wanted to hear everything that Alex said this time, they wanted to listen to his voice. I did not tell him because it would have made natural conversation almost impossible, and he had enough to worry about.

The next day I only saw him at the offices of the Scientific

Research Committee when I went for my interview. It was strange to be back at the long green baize table. Levin was there but most of the others had changed. Levin greeted me with cordial formality. He said he hoped I had enjoyed the Soviet Fair in Paris and I congratulated him on a magnificent Soviet achievement. I could see no suspicion in his eyes. It was a short meeting and my proposals about the mobile exhibition were politely accepted pending an accurate timetable. The room looked just the same. The windows were still dirty. Alex said very little, and I thought how different he looked to when I had first seen him sitting at this table before we knew each other. Surely the others could see the difference? But maybe he said it was the baby keeping him awake at nights.

That evening I dined alone. Alex thought it best for us not to be seen too much in public. My visa was only for three days, and we had arranged to meet on the next and last evening at the Peking restaurant. We never went twice running to the same restaurant. I did not enjoy my lonely dinner. Moscow without Alex seemed empty and hostile, and I did not like what he had told me.

Next night I was a little early at the Peking. There was a fair crowd in the street. I could not tell whether I was being watched, but it was bad to be seen hanging about, so I walked up and down the opposite pavement till I saw Alex approaching the Peking. He carried a briefcase. I crossed the road but instead of greeting me, he went straight into the foyer. I knew that something must be very wrong. When I followed he still made no sign of recognition but glanced inside the restaurant, then turned and as he passed me whispered, 'Follow behind.' He walked quickly down the street and, when he came to an alleyway leading to some tenements, he dodged out of sight. I turned in after him and he grabbed my arm and said, 'You must get out, quickly! You are being followed. Be at the airport tomorrow by six o'clock. I'll be there.' Then he was gone down the alley and I went back into the street.

As I came out of the alley I saw two men. They did not stop me, but later in Lubyanka I saw the photographs they had taken.

Back at the Ukraine Hotel I asked the female clerk in my corridor for the room key. She said, 'No key—administration.' I tried the door but it was locked. I was suspicious. Administration were on the ground floor. They did not keep the room keys. I asked the woman again, and she said, 'Administration—*please*,' so I went down, and was kept waiting about a quarter of an hour, but no one had my key.

Up again to the corridor, and now the woman was all smiles: 'Your key—I find him.'

Alone in my room, I saw at once that it had been searched. I always folded my shirts and handkerchiefs in a special way, and they had been moved. On my bathroom shelf were packets of washing soap and cleaning powder, among them the tin of Harpic which was to appear at the trial. The tin had a false bottom for concealing film. We had never used the tin, but later in Lubyanka I was shown a photograph of it lying on my hotel bed with all my personal belongings. Now in the bedroom everything was back in place. The film which Alex had given me on the first morning was still in my pocket.

I was booked on the noon flight next morning but, as Alex instructed, I was at the airport by six o'clock.

For almost an hour I hung about, and suddenly someone touched my arm, and there was Alex.

'We've got to put you on the first plane to the West,' he said, 'there's no time to lose.'

He told me what had happened the night before. His briefcase had contained vital material. When he saw that the Peking restaurant was being watched, he went down the street to the alleyway. As he turned in, he dropped the envelope behind a post. This was the safety drill which he had decided beforehand. If he had been arrested with that envelope, his story would have ended then and there.

Later that night he collected the envelope, which he gave to me now.

The earliest flight for me was the 9.15 to Copenhagen.

Alex used his security card and his still strong authority to hasten my ticket transfer. By coming he took a terrible risk, but without him I would never have made it. Even with him, I had only half an hour to spare. He looked at the end of his tether, grim, chain-smoking, very worried. When the flight was called, he gave me a long bulky envelope.

'Look after it. It's the best.'

'Don't worry. I'll look after it.'

'Tell my friends that I must come out, soon, very soon. I will try to carry on, but it's very dangerous.'

He came with me to the aircraft. There were no delays on take-off, and as we moved away I saw Alex wave from the tarmac. It was not a big wave, just his hand raised once above his head.

# 5

# Release

ALEX is waving from the tarmac. He has got me on to the early plane. He may have risked his life by doing this. Why is the air in here so cold and sweet? My lungs are full of it. Where is Alex? He has gone. Where am I? This is not an aircraft, it is all dark, I can see nothing.

I see nothing because my eyes are closed. When I open them, I find that I am on my bed in Vladimir. The woman doctor is putting the oxygen mask back on the trolley. Then she bends over me and my arm feels the sharp jab of a needle.

So they would not let me die! That is my first thought, and it changes everything, it means that whatever happens to me, whatever they do, I am separated and distinct from other prisoners. With my next meal I get some Bovril and vitamin tablets which Sheila had sent me. I am kept in bed and each day I have an injection and my food improves, I have meat, not what you would call meat but a small occasional cube floating in the fish soup, I have milk and some white bread. Books too and some magazines from England (with the advertisements cut out, lest the guards should see the degrading luxury of Western civilisation with its Hoovers and washing machines and expensive cars) and some paper and a pencil to write home.

But the great fact is that I was not allowed to die. I am

still weak and scraggy, with no power in my hands, and when after a week in bed I am given my first outing in the exercise pen, I almost faint when I stand up. But I am alive and shall be kept alive, my tiny night-light flame is shielded and shall not be blown out.

I am quietly content with my new status, when the door opens and I have a cell-mate, a weedy and repulsive Russian youth, and I presume we are back on the pumping routine. As with George, I cannot pronounce his Russian name, so I call him Max. From the first moment I dislike him. For George, with his frostbite and his podgy frame, I had a certain affection, but for Max I have none. His eyes are close together and there is a whine in his voice. The thought of sharing the oil-drum with Max revolts me. I complain to the warden, and the warden tells me to put in a written complaint to Chevshenko, and I write, and nothing happens, and I decide to get rid of Max myself. I calculate the best way is assault. It will indeed be a puny battle for Max is hardly more robust than I am, but someone might trip and a skull be banged against the wall, and I feel sure that whatever they think of Max, they will wish my skull to be kept intact for its possible revelations. So one morning I fly at Max and squawk a war-cry as I punch his stomach, and we have hardly begun our grapple before the guard roars in to separate us, and Max is taken away.

Now my crosses tell me it is February. The cold, like everything else in the Soviet landscape, is immense, and my diet, though above the death-level, gives me little resistance. Since my collapse, interrogations have ceased, and I am bored with the long cold nights and the short cold days. Sometimes an immense wind blows and I am glad to be inside. Through my spy-hole I can see the white frozen compound, I see the working parties moving off in the morning, the lines of shuffling derelicts in their tattered greatcoats, and in the evening I see them come back exhausted, slipping and staggering on the frozen snow. I see the prison walls and beyond them nothing but the huge dull sky, a sheet of lead on which the sun, looking peculiarly small and neat, rises and falls in a pitiful arc, never very high, yellow all day and red towards sunset. I look forward to my daily exercise, except that from the pen I can hear much coughing and spewing, and the funeral band plays more often than in summer, and when for no special reason my oil-drum is withdrawn and I am allowed for a few days to go to the lavatory myself, I almost resent this privilege because of the slimy cough-blood on the floor, and I hope the doctor has some good injections for tuberculosis, and as I crouch down and look at the observation hole in the locked door, I see an eye watching me and hear a cackle of high-pitched laughter.

I am brought to the wash-house and lavatory by a male guard, but the females are often hanging about, and when they have nothing better to do they stand and jeer while I am sluicing my naked body, and afterwards they come and stare at me through the hole in the lavatory door and make jokes which I am sure are coarse.

My doubtful privilege only lasts a week, and then I am back with my oil-drum in the cell. In the daytime it is cold, but at nights there is a penetrating iciness in the air which floods into my bones and makes the steel pin in my hip feel like a dentist's drill in a bad tooth. I put sheets of *Pravda* across my chest and stomach and round my feet, but my scalp and toes still feel frozen solid, and as I lie listening to the wind and shielding my eyes from the strong hard light over the door, I concentrate on the meat and milk I have swallowed today, and try to persuade my stomach how fortunate it is.

The fortune does not last very long, less than a fortnight.

One morning Chevshenko sends for me. The interpreter stands respectfully, and Chevshenko sprawls as he always sprawls, fat, unshaven, dirty, and venomous. He says, 'I see you are still alive,' which sounds promising, but then he adds, 'so you will appreciate what is going to happen to you unless you tell us the truth instead of these stupid lies. We have decided to show you what Vladimir can be like for those who do not co-operate. I hope you will come to your senses—while there is still time.' He looks up at me with his heavy bloodshot eyes.

So now it is goodbye to my books and paper and pencil. My cigarettes are stopped, the meat disappears from my soup, my milk vanishes and my bread turns from white to knubbly black. My exercise is cut to twice a week and I am not allowed to shave. The old blow-hot-blow-cold routine is introduced, but now I do not care. Disappointment is an emotion I have long since ceased to feel. When a food parcel from home is brought into the cell, chocolate and Marmite and cigarettes and Nescafé, and I sign for having received it, and the parcel is immediately taken away, I feel nothing because I expect nothing. Every few days I go before Chevshenko, and he rages and threatens, and I repeat that I have told all I know and have no more to say, and I remember that they will not let me die. Not intentionally. But sometimes, waking in the small hours, I have a frozen fear that perhaps they will miscalculate the food that is necessary, and the small guttering flame in the saucer will suddenly run dry, and I shall just cease, quietly and without warning.

In England we do not understand what winter really means, but in Vladimir I understand. When I look through my spy-hole and see the cold trudging prisoners moving one slow leg after another, certain to die, if not this winter then the next or the next, simply because they are too cold to live, I see why primitive peoples worshipped the sun which warms the bodies and warms the soil to give the bodies food, I see why all religions, no matter what their creeds of behaviour, celebrate the spring when the seeds of food are planted and the autumn when the food is harvested, I see why Christmas

comes not exactly upon but just after the shortest day of the
year, for now the death of the year is over, and now, clearly,
is the moment for the birth of life.

Soviet prisoners will rarely, if ever, leave Vladimir alive.
If they finish their sentence, they will be given another. The
only sure thing that awaits them is a hole in the ground. In
winter the hole will be frozen and in summer it will be muddy,
so what is the difference? Why do they stagger round the
pens and make their small sad jokes to each other and risk being beaten black and blue for a cigarette and rot in their cells?
What do they hope for when there is no hope? Why don't
they just die, quickly? There is no answer, no explanation.
The force of life is blind, it does not understand the meaning
of hopelessness.

Blow hot, blow cold. My cigarettes have been stopped, but
one day the deputy warden asks me with a twisted smile
whether I would like some tobacco, and I reply without the
slightest expression of face or voice that if he wishes me to
have tobacco, I shall be pleased to have it. He gives an order,
and the guard throws down a packet of Russian tobacco.
The packet is made of brown paper with the word 'Mowcopka' in scrawly letters. The tobacco is the dry and dusty
scrapings from the root of the plant. The deputy warden
knows that I have no cigarette papers or holder because they
have been taken away. He leaves me, pleased no doubt at my
frustration.

The question is how to get a smoke. Dust or not, it is better
than nothing. And the answer is not so difficult as the deputy
warden imagines, for one of the few treasures which I have
managed to save through all the confiscations is a pencil
(bought in W. H. Smith's at Sloane Square) with a rubber
fixed to the end by a metal tube. The tube shall be my holder,
and now all I have to do is to roll a small piece of *Pravda*, insert the roll into the tube, and fill the roll with Mowcopka.
Now I have my cigarette. To light it, I pull some flock out of

my mattress, roll the flock into a ball, and vigorously rub the ball with my shoe on the gritty floor. Soon the smouldering begins, I can light my cigarette, and now I am puffing away and thinking about the deputy warden.

I make the Mowcopka last a week. It is soothing to the nerves but foul for the stomach. Three Mowcopkas running and I start to vomit. Now it is March, and I am very weak again, almost back to the light-headed listlessness of the days before I collapsed. Chevshenko rants and raves at me and, although I refuse to stand smartly to attention, I still have to stand, and sometimes I am afraid that I shall fall down in the middle of interrogation, and it is only my contempt of Chevshenko that keeps me on my feet.

I have been in captivity for over sixteen months, and when I subtract sixteen months from five years I am appalled at the remainder. It is useless to make plans for facing another three years and eight months, the only hope is to face each day as it comes. If I collapse again, they will revive me, that is certain. I shall have another week in bed with the meat cubes and the Marmite. They dare not let me die. I shall get through— as long as they do not miscalculate! But what are the chances? I see the guard looking at me in a strange way, as one looks at a freak in a side show. The human wraith! The living skeleton! Roll up, roll up! But here it is I who have miscalculated, for one morning there is a ferocious bang on my door, and the guard's scowling face appears at the trap and starts hollering as if I have committed some number one misdemeanour. I do not understand a word of what he is shouting, but by the way he jerks his head, I gather that there are other guards in the corridor, and before I can guess what is going on, he winks at me and suddenly his left hand shoots through the trap in the door, and I see he is holding out a salami sandwich. From now on, almost every day he comes and thunders at me, for the benefit of the other guards, and brings me food, pieces of meat and bars of chocolate. I smile and nod, but he does not smile back, he just gives me food. He is my inscrutable saviour.

It is the act almost more than the food which sustains me. I do not often feel gratitude in Vladimir, and the feeling does me good. When I am trotting in figures of eight round the frozen pen, my stomach deals thankfully with the chocolate and I think gratefully about the guard with his scowling Slav face and his kind left hand. The chocolate and meat give me that extra morsel of energy which allows me to enjoy my exercise and not to feel frightened by the wind. Since Christmas, off and on, the immense Soviet wind has blown over Vladimir. It is not like the English wind which turns umbrellas inside out, or lifts off a thatch or two, or lashes the waves over Brighton Parade. The wind that passes over the vast plain at Vladimir seems to have come from further away, to be travelling faster and more savagely than any wind you ever felt in England. Through the spy-hole in the cell you see the air filled suddenly with a haze of powdered snow, you see the tottering party of prisoners huddle together like leaves blown into a pile in the gutter, you feel that if the wind really decided, it could pick up one of the leaves and blow it to Vladivostok.

But now in mid-March the wind grows less savage, makes less noise at nights, and the coldness seems minutely less cold. My hip stops throbbing in bed, and one morning in the exercise pen I am startled by a thump behind me, and I see that a wad of snow has fallen from the wall. For a few days there are small moments of thaw followed by more freezing, there seems to be a meteorological indecision, and then suddenly the compound is glistening wet and the great melt is on the way.

Now the immense snow becomes the immense slush, and hardly have I apprehended that winter is really over, when I am taken once more to Lubyanka. As usual my luggage comes with me, but this time I am given my civilian suit in

Vladimir and I travel not in a railway truck but in a curtained car with the prison warden and two guards. It is the same journey, in reverse, that I made so long ago when I came to Vladimir, and once more I look through the windscreen and see the vast flat slushy landscape. I am much weaker now, and the journey seems endless, but as soon as we reach Lubyanka I am given a meal with some meat and a little milk, and I wonder what this improvement may signify. But I do not wonder much because I am beyond speculation.

For two days I get the extra food, and some vitamin pills, and on the third day I am told that my wife is in Moscow and I am taken to meet her in the Supreme Court building.

The warden from Lubyanka is with me and when we come into the room I see Sheila and my defence counsel, Borovik, standing beside her. I see a look almost of horror on Sheila's face. Long afterwards she told me that she hardly recognised this gaunt and sickly creature. But now quickly she pulls herself together and greets me, and I notice that Borovik too has a shocked expression in his eyes, and I say to him, 'Well, Mr. Borovik, see me now. Are you *proud* of yourself?'

I do not have long with Sheila and we do not speak of Vladimir, we speak of home and our friends and Andrew, but she keeps looking at me as if she longs to pass me some of her own strength, and in the middle of our chat she slips in, 'I'm not sure, but I think things are happening; it's possible there will be some good news before very long.' I do not pay too much attention to this. I have seen the look in her eyes and I think she is trying to encourage me because I look so awful.

The next morning I am taken for interrogation. There is yet another new Russian general and two interpreters, and the other interrogators are nationals from the satellite countries, from everywhere except Poland. For a week the interrogations continue. Who were my contacts? Who are these people in the photograph? Whom did I meet at this and that hotel?

I do not know. That is not correct. There was no one. I have never seen this man.

By the end of the week the General is getting very loud and nasty. I am ordered to sign a document saying that I confess to being an agent and also that I am willing to work for the Soviets. If I do not sign, they say, a tape-recording will be played over Moscow Radio. The tape is played to me. It has been faked from the conversation I had long ago in London, when Kulikov was making his sly proposals. Now my words have been cut and rearranged to mean that I am ready to do what he asks. I am told that if I do not sign, they will tell the whole world how I have betrayed not only Penkovsky but also the British people, how I offered to work as a double agent for the Soviets.

But I do not sign, and soon I am back in my cell at Vladimir, back to prison uniform, back to Chevshenko.

For a few days he uses all his old sarcastic threats, and I am preparing myself for another long spell of Chevshenko beastliness when another bed is brought into my cell, and here is my third cell-mate.

He is a Russian and the best of the three. I call him Charles. He speaks quite fluent English with a deep throaty accent. He does not have body odour and frostbitten hands like George, and compared with the repulsive Max he is almost a gentleman. He has a tired worldly face, and although I do not propose to trust him to the extent of saying anything that the interrogators would like to hear, I do not object to a game of draughts, nor to the mild improvement in food. We are allowed a few books and magazines, and I listen to the sad tale of how Charles was caught in the Black Market.

He was manager of a grocery store, it seems, in Gorky Street. One of his chief consignments was lemons from Georgia. The lemons would arrive by the wagon load, and when Charles saw that he would never grow rich on the profits which the State allowed him, he hatched the simple and effective idea of ordering six wagons of lemons, but only putting five through his books. The sixth had, of course, to be paid for, but the profit, instead of being shared in most unjust proportions between him and the State, was now all his own.

At first all went well and Charles dreamed of a magnificent future, but one day there was a breakdown on the line and the wagons were stranded miles away. For weeks the precious lemons remained beyond his reach, and when at last the authorities opened the wagons, they found the lemons all mouldy. Enquiries revealed the errors in Charles's books, and he was given fifteen years.

Charles stayed with me over a month, with never a quarrel and many a mile together in figures of eight round the exercise pens. Sometimes for several days we are left together, then I am taken for a session with Chevshenko, then back to Charles. He tries in a half-hearted way to pump me, but soon gives it up. I guess he is telling them that he needs time to work on me, so that they will let him stay, for I think he enjoys our strange sad little comradeship. All prisoners, no matter where they come from, are comrades. Instinctively they help each other, they plot together, as Charles plots with me over the incident of the singing women, one of the last and most touching of all my Vladimir memories.

In the hospital block, as I have said, the doorway leading out to the pens is in the middle of the bottom row of cells where the women prisoners live. They do not live, they exist with a starved frailty even more terrible than the frailty of the men, they are liable to the same punishment as the men, the loss of food, the beatings, the days or weeks in black dungeons with planks to sleep on, and then only for a few hours.

These women are deeply religious. Some are in Vladimir because they believe in God, like the woman who started a

Sunday school in Kharkov and is now serving twenty years. Their belief is indestructible, the last and only thing which keeps them alive, and, because they cannot pray together, they sing together in cracked and quavering voices the hymns and chants remembered from happier days. It is forbidden, but they do it. They are punished, but they do it. The only way to stop them singing would be to kill them. Sometimes, coming or going to the pens, we see the cropped heads and wizened faces bobbing up at the fanlight windows, and one starts to sing and others join in, and the ghastly carol floats up out of the line of cells from which they will never escape.

In one of my magazines, a copy of the *Illustrated London News*, I discover a full-page coloured photograph of the consecration of Coventry Cathedral. Light through the stained glass windows falls on the great golden cross. It is a splendid study, full of peace and grandeur, and I feel sure it will help the women if only they can see it. They cannot read the title, and probably few if any have ever been in a cathedral, but they will know what it is, the message will surely get through.

The problem is how to pass the photograph.

First I tear the page out, then I fold it carefully till it is small enough to conceal in my hand with a pellet of soap for extra weight. I plan to throw the packet through an open fanlight, but I know the guard will be watching, so I need Charles's help. We discuss and rehearse our parts.

Our exercise today is in the afternoon, and when we reach the doorway the guard goes ahead and wheels round to face us as we come out. The nearest window is only a few feet away, and it is at this moment that Charles trips and bends down to fumble with his shoe. The guard, as we hoped, jumps forward and leans over Charles to see what is happening, and in a flash I turn and flip the packet, which rises agonisingly into the air and falls into the cell.

Nothing more happens today but by next afternoon the news has been passed, perhaps in the wash-house, even the picture itself has been passed from hand to hand, the beautiful coloured picture of the House of God. As Charles and I come through the doorway, a small shrunken face appears at the window and the singing begins, the chant which is taken up at the top of every thin voice from every cell, and faces appear, and those who can't climb up wave hands like bird-claws through the window flap, and Charles and I trot round the pen listening to the heartrending paean of thanks, the song of freedom sung by slaves.

Not long after this, Charles, having failed in his task, is withdrawn like his predecessors, and a few days later I am told once more to sort out my luggage and put on civilian clothes. I do not try to guess where I am going, it is probably to Lubyanka, but for no special reason except that Chevshenko was particularly aggressive this morning, I decide to vary my departure with a little confusion. I am allowed a shower, after which I am supposed to place my prison uniform on a pile of others, but it is very cold today and, when the guard's back is turned, I slip into my uniform again and put my civilian shirt and suit on top. I even manage to pop my prison mug and spoon into a suitcase. These crimes are bound to be discovered, and if I come back to Vladimir I shall be punished, but I do not care. This particular guard is a bastard, and Chevshenko is another, and my mind, feeble and obstinate, thinks only of confusion and not of consequences.

A car is waiting, and I am driven on the old long trail to Lubyanka, and after three days of waiting for what I expect to be more interrogation, I am taken instead to the airport, and before I know what is happening, we are airborne in a clear sky. No one tells me anything, no one even speaks to me. Naturally I wonder where I am going, and my first thought is that perhaps I am being taken to one of the satellite countries for further interrogation, to Czechoslovakia or Hungary, but as time goes on, and since I have nothing to read, I begin to do some calculations. I am no navigator and I have no watch, but I know roughly what the time is and I can see the sun, which is on the port side, and basing my sums on the fact that if we were flying due West the sun at midday would be on the port beam, I decide, with many clumsy allowances, that we are indeed flying in a westerly direction—which is not the way to the Balkans! They are much further round towards the south. There is only one likely place I can think of which lies roughly west from Moscow, and now a very strange thought enters my mind, a thought too enormous to be taken seriously. I stop my calculations because I dare not entertain the hope which they arouse, but when at last we touch down, the first thing I see is a sign in German, and I know that I was right, that we have landed in East Germany.

A car takes me to the Red Army barracks, where I meet the Soviet Consul. He speaks good English. He tells me that some money, about £30, which my wife sent to me in prison, is now to be returned to me, but not in cash. For form's sake I protest, though I do not care about the money, but the Consul is politely firm. He insists on knowing what I would like instead of my money, and I say 'Caviare?'[1]

That night I sleep under heavy guard in a requisitioned house. I am woken in the small hours, given a good breakfast, and by dawn I am sitting between two hefty guards in a car which takes me out into the country. We stop beside a shed, that is all I can see. For over an hour we sit in silence, then the Consul comes to the window of the car and says: 'You are going round there. If you speak or misbehave you will be shot.'

---

1. I got three dozen tins. When I opened them later, it was mouldy.

The car moves round the shed and I see we are at a frontier. I get out of the car. The men hold my arms tightly. There are soldiers everywhere with dogs and rifles and binoculars. A telescope is mounted on a tripod.

Through the gates is a small piece of no-man's-land. At the far side another car draws up and stops. One man from that side and one from this march solemnly towards each other, stop, converse, and march on to make their identification. The man approaching me wears a white mackintosh. As he comes near, I recognise him! Alex would have recognised him! I am identified by this man from the West, and the man from the East identifies whoever is waiting over there.

At last, after endless mute hand-signals, I am marched to the middle of the no-man's-land, where I meet the prisoner from the West. The exchange is made, and now I pass on to the West and he to the East. I know who this man is. He is a Russian spy, who operated under the name of Lonsdale. He looks sleek, well fed, and needs a hair-cut, but then he has not been in the Soviet Union for a long time.

He is welcome to it.

I too have a welcome. First by the R.A.F. station commander and his wife who offer me a hot bath and a wonderful breakfast, then by five of my old colleagues who are waiting downstairs, among them (of all people!) James himself, who greets me with truly British enthusiasm: 'Greville! You look bloody 'orrible!'

It is hard to believe that I am back with James and his friends, that I am safe. I can still hardly believe it when I am alone in the aircraft heading for England. I know it is true, but a heaviness weighs on me when I think that here I am, at the end of it all, flying to safety, while Alex is still there, alive or dead. I do not know which, but I know he will never escape.

My mind goes back to the autumn of 1962, when I took the Mobile Exhibition to Budapest in the hope of paving the way to rescue Alex. In fact, as I learnt later at the trial, Alex was arrested eleven days before they arrested me, so that my journey was useless. But I did not know this at the time, and if I had the journey to make again, knowing only what I then knew, I would still make it.

In late September 1962 the Mobile Exhibition was ready for its maiden trip. We were too late for Leningrad, but there was a Trade Fair in Bucharest which gave us an excuse for going to the Balkans, and I planned to call in at Budapest and try to arrange a private exhibition there. It was important not to be tied to official fairs, I had to establish myself as an independent unit if I were ever to get to the Soviet Union with a chance of rescuing Alex.

The caravans had been built to my own design. The two vehicles together were sixty-five feet long, twelve high, and eight wide. Each vehicle had two main compartments, and for an exhibition the side flaps dropped down and the compartments, each lined in a different wood and with anodised aluminium ceilings, became showrooms measuring twenty feet by ten, where tools and machinery were on display. For the reception outside we had stanchions which held a boundary of white rope, and tall parasols for the coffee tables, and a natty pair of steps up to the showrooms. There were projectors for slides and films, and hung in the space between the vehicles was a typists' office with electric typewriters and tape-recorders. Foreign visitors could be fetched from the airport in a Mini (painted with a Union Jack) which was housed in the back of the trailer. We could stow enough liquor for a battalion and, if our guests wanted hot drinks or snacks, we had a small kitchen aft of the driver's cabin where there was a stove heated either by Calor gas or electricity, a fridge, a washing machine, a spin dryer, and under the sink a sixty-gallon slop-bin, so that we could hold the dirty water and empty it later on the open road.

In transit, the driver had world-wide short-wave radio to keep him happy. At night curtains pulled across the windscreen, his seat became a bed, and there were two more in the small conference room next to the kitchen. There was power steering, automatic lubrication, a six kilowatt generating plant with stabilised voltage, and enough diesel in the tanks to last four hundred miles without refuelling.

Thirty-five thousand pounds' worth of beauty!

British Intelligence maintained on the whole their usual enthusiastic silence, but James became for once really voluble when, having examined every inch of the vehicles inside and out, he muttered:

'I see you've forgotten the vital thing.'

'What's that?'

'The bidet.'

We were the largest unit ever seen on British roads. After a trial trip to the Midlands, our route heralded and cleared by the police, we gave a farewell party to friends and trade representatives in the car park of the Festival Hall, and then set out, on a day of glorious sunshine, for our journey across Europe.

My two drivers took the caravans, and I went ahead by car to arrange frontier clearance and parking sites.

We rendezvoused in Vienna, where I had been told to call in case there were any last minute instructions or news of Alex. There was none, and we went to Budapest and were met by my manager who took the caravans on to Bucharest, while I stayed behind to arrange the private exhibition.

I had been often to Hungary and had always enjoyed myself, but I did not enjoy myself now.

In Budapest, when the caravans had gone on, I set about my enquiries, but it was not the same rather lazy old-fashioned Budapest as before. There was a depressing bustle and glumness, and for me personally an encounter which at once set all my alarm bells ringing.

I hardly booked in to the Duna Hotel when the chief clerk pounced on me and introduced a dark wavy-haired young man to whom I took an immediate dislike. 'This is Mr. Ambrus. He is a student and an excellent interpreter. He could be of much help to you.'

'I have seen your Mobile Exhibition,' said Ambrus. 'It is very fine. We hope it will come here after Bucharest.'

I did not want an interpreter, I already had one, a pretty Hungarian girl called Helen Serespyen who had worked with me before, but Helen was not always available and I could not object to Ambrus without creating suspicion, so I said I would be pleased to have a second interpreter because if we had an exhibition there would be a big crowd of visitors. But how did Ambrus know about Bucharest? I had only corresponded officially with the Hungarian Trade Minister.

It took me several days to arrange the exhibition. I was interviewed by the head of the British section of the Budapest Chamber of Commerce and, after an unnecessarily large number of questions, since my business activities were well known in Budapest, I was told that permission would be given for Hungarian representatives to attend my exhibition here when it had finished in Bucharest.

All the time I was worried about Ambrus. He was always waiting when I came down in the morning, always ready to come with me wherever I was going. He was too ready. He explained that he was waiting to obtain work in the Tourist Bureau, but it would be next season before there was anything much to do, in the meantime he was at my service, and what did I require? To be shot of you, I thought. But there was no way to get rid of him, and he trailed round with me whenever he could. One morning he said, 'I have a funny story to tell you, about someone who tried to escape from Budapest . . .' but I cut him short by saying, 'I don't wish to hear about such things.' I did not like anything about Ambrus. When I came downstairs he would be sitting so solemn and sly in the chair, and when he saw me he would jump up with his face creased in a smile and his eyes as cold as a cod.

It was not only Ambrus who upset me. Several times when I drove towards the city boundary my car was followed, and I only lost the tail when I turned back. This looked as if they wanted to be sure I would not flit without warning. Again, when I went for a night to Lake Balaton, I was told on arrival at the hotel that my room, which I had booked, was not available. Another hotel was waiting for me. I did not like the sound of a strange hotel chosen by the Hungarians. Who might be waiting to receive me? So I found accommodation for myself and returned to Budapest next day.

Driving through the plains I saw massive troop movements and lines of armoured vehicles and tanks. It was clear that the Cuban crisis, blowing to its climax on the other side of the world, was being taken very seriously here. The Balkans, under Soviet instruction, were undoubtedly preparing for possible war.

When I had finished my arrangements, I decided to go back to the safety of Vienna and think things over. There was still no news of Alex, and certainly no chance of getting to the Soviet Union this trip. My manager could run the Exhibition in Budapest, and if necessary I could be taken ill in Vienna and not return. It was not the best way of doing things, but I had a feeling of personal danger, and each day the feeling got stronger.

I organised my departure as if I intended to return for the Exhibition, asking the hotel if I might leave two suitcases. To prevent any suspicion when I left, I carried only a briefcase to the car. As soon as I had passed the frontier and was among the quiet friendly villages of Austria I felt a lot better, but I wondered what they were thinking in Budapest.

At Vienna I garaged the car and made a telephone call to a special number in London. I asked about 'our friend in the other place' and was told that he was still sending reports. Reassured about Alex, I explained in code language about my suspicions in Budapest. I was asked to carry on acting normally, so I took a plane to Bucharest in time for the Trade Fair. The Mobile Exhibition was a great success, but everything was overshadowed by the news that, after a final clash between Kennedy and Khrushchev, a Soviet ship had been stopped in the Atlantic on its way to Cuba and had been sent home. Everyone was talking about this, there was a tremendous feeling that war had been averted, and I wondered if Alex realised how much that last vital envelope had contributed to peace, what strength it had given to Kennedy in his dealings with Khrushchev.

A few days before the Fair was over, I went by air to Vienna to pick up the car.

That evening an extraordinary thing happened.

Passing the hotel desk I was given an envelope with my name scrawled in capital letters. Inside was a sheet of cheap paper with the words, again in capitals, 'PLEASE COME TO OPERA AT TEN. *PLEASE.*' There was no signature.

My first thought was that this was a trap. They had been sent from Budapest to get me. But surely not. It was too crude. If they had really wanted to take me, they would have done it more smoothly, I would have received some phoney invitation to the Embassy, a car would have been waiting, and they would have found a writer who knew enough English not to leave out the definite article. Besides, although I had certainly been suspicious, I had not done anything suspicious, except perhaps to leave Budapest, and they could hardly arrest me for that, especially when I had promised to return. So at five minutes to ten I walked through the streets to the square in front of the Opera House. The doors were open and the foyer brightly lit. It must have been an interval, for as I got nearer, people began to come out and stand on the steps. This reassured me again, it would have been a silly time and place to organise a snatch.

Slowly I walked up to the entrance, ready to run for my life. No one spoke to me or stopped me. I stood among the opera-goers with my back to the wall and lit a cigarette. For a minute or two nothing happened, and I was about to go away when a girl's breathless voice spoke my name, and I turned, and stared, and could not think where I had seen her before—but of course! It was Sonja!

I asked her what she was doing in Vienna and she said she was on holiday, but she seemed desperately nervous and I did not believe her.

'How did you know I was here, and my hotel?' I said.

'I see you—in the street. You go into hotel.'

It sounded most unlikely. 'So—what do you want, Sonja?'

She looked at me with real agony in her eyes and said: 'Do you know—where is Alex?'

'If you want to speak to me of Alex,' I said, 'you must tell my why you are in Vienna. You did not come here for a holiday, I am sure of that.'

Sonja stuck to her story. She stood twisting her hands together, glancing around, and suddenly I realised the truth. They had sent her because she knew me, she was here to point me out to Soviet agents in Vienna. I felt sure that at this very moment we were being watched by Soviet agents; this meeting was in fact an identification parade, which, though she had been ordered to arrange the meeting, she was using for her own purpose, to ask about Alex.

It was an interesting thought but there was no need to be cruel, so I told her that I had not seen Alex for a long time. At this she almost burst into tears. She did not use the word 'love', but this, clearly, was what it was all about. They had been friends in Paris, they had written to each other afterwards, and now for a long time her letters had been un-answered. I remembered what Alex had said on the last time

in Moscow—'She got too serious'—but now she was dis-
traught, so I told her that, when I saw him again, I would
mention her, and she nodded with a sad little smile and left
me as suddenly as she had come.

I hurried back to telephone London, but it was Friday
evening and the phone was not manned, so I rang my wife
and asked her to fly out next morning. It was essential to
have a messenger, should I decide that London must know
my latest news.

When she arrived and we were sitting peacefully on the
hotel terrace in the autumn sunshine, I had a strong impulse
to pack our bags and drive straight back to England with
her. I had never, of course, told her about my work, but I
had never been so near to telling. I could perhaps have given
her a letter to post, whose address would have meant nothing
and whose contents she would never have known. But she
had a heavy cold, and was telling me that Andrew also had
not been well, and I decided not to burden her with a re-
sponsibility that could never be hers. If she had posted a letter in London I would have had to wait for a reply, and this
would have detained me in Vienna where I was already under
observation by Russian agents. I remembered grimly that
when Alex had asked me in Paris whether he should go or
stay, I had replied that it was up to him. Well, now it was up
to me, there was no shoulder to lean on, no one could decide
for me. There was no compulsion, I was not being ordered
to go, it was entirely for me to judge as I thought best.

Sunday, the day of peace, was a day of torment. I was so
keyed up I could hardly eat, and I had to force myself to be
relaxed and pleasant with Sheila, who after all had crossed
Europe to be with me. As we strolled down the Kärtner-
strasse I felt the thoughts hammering inside my head till I
was surprised she could not hear them.

On Monday Sheila flew back to England, and I had to

make my decision. I did not want to go to Budapest, every instinct warned me to stay, but the inescapable fact was that if I were not present at my own first private exhibition, this would prejudice my chances of forming a pattern which might later allow me to reach Alex in the Soviet Union.

Many times on the frontier I almost turned back, but once the frontier was passed I drove quickly on towards Budapest. This was the 22nd October, the day they took Alex, but I drove on, ignorant in the sunshine. In the Hotel Duna the first person I met was Ambrus.

He greeted me warmly, and I had hardly put down my cases when he was saying tomorrow he would like me to meet his grandmother and grandfather, they lived on an island in the Danube outside the city, it was very quiet and picturesque, they would be delighted to make my acquaintance. I did not care for the idea of islands in quiet places, so I said it would depend on my appointments, but Ambrus knew that I had no appointment next morning and suggested ten o'clock, and I said, 'Very well, then, ten o'clock,' but early the next day I telephoned a business friend, and when I found Ambrus at ten, I was able to say truthfully that I would have to make it another time.

When I came back to the hotel at two o'clock, there was Ambrus. I asked him out for lunch, and he said, 'There's a nice place near the ferry where we can lunch, and then you can come and see my grandparents.'

I said: 'All right, we can have lunch near the ferry. I don't know whether I shall have time to see your grandparents. We shall have to see when the ferry goes.'

I took him in my car, and in the quiet country outside the city he told me to drive down a narrow road towards the river. Through the trees I could see an old house, but no ferry. I said that the bumpy road was bad for my car, and stopped, and Ambrus got out and started bawling in Hungarian. I asked him what he was doing, and he said he was calling the ferryman, and presently an old man came through the trees, and Ambrus gabbled to him for quite a while, and I reversed the car back to the main road. When Ambrus joined me I said it was getting later than I had thought, and I preferred to return to the city for lunch.

For the next week he kept reminding me about his grand-parents who were so keenly awaiting my visit, but I put him off by saying I was too busy getting ready for the Exhibition on Friday.

And now it is Friday the 2nd November, and all day I am busy with my drivers setting up the caravans in Varosliget Park. We plan to open the Exhibition with a cocktail party at five o'clock. The manager of the Duna Hotel organises the food and drink, and I see that everything is spick and span in the caravans. The party itself will take place in the Pavilion, and the caravans are set up under the trees nearby.

It is a splendid party. There is plenty of liquor, and long tables covered with tasty snacks, and many representatives from Hungarian business houses. The Hungarians are great drinkers, and I take them in twos and threes to the caravans, and then back to the liquor. There are many toasts and com-pliments, and still plenty of drinking time left, when sud-denly, at about seven o'clock, the Hungarians all melt away, as if on order, and I am left alone with Ambrus among the empty bottle-laden tables.

As we come down the Pavilion steps, there is a pale light in the sky and a great stillness. I feel overwhelmingly the sense of danger that I have felt since the first moment I set eyes on Ambrus. I can see my caravans not a hundred yards away under the trees, and I know I shall never reach them.

Now, it is all over. I am in the aircraft, coming in to land at Northolt.

There is a sea of friendly faces, but still the most important welcome is ahead and at last, on the evening of this miraculous day, it comes, the welcome of all welcomes.

I am home.

## *Greville Wynne*

Greville Wynne was born in Shropshire, England, in 1919. After his university studies, he qualified as an electrical engineer and entered the world of commerce. For the past twenty years he has been Director of his own firm, Industrial Sales Consultants. His work for British Intelligence during World War II led to his more recent Intelligence activities for the British and American services, as described in this book. Mr. Wynne has traveled extensively in eastern and western Europe, and since his release from a Russian prison in exchange for the Soviet spy Gordon Lansdale he has visited Canada and the United States. He lives in London with his wife and son.